FOR ORGANS, PIANOS & ELECTRONIC KEYBOARDS

E-Z PLAY TODAY

328

FRENCH SONGS

CONTENTS

ISBN 978-1-4234-3622-5

HAL•LEONARD®
CORPORATION

7777 W. BLUEMOUND RD. P.O. BOX 13819 MILWAUKEE, WI 53213

Visit Hal Leonard Online at
www.halleonard.com

April in Paris

Registration 2
Rhythm: Fox Trot or Swing

Words by E.Y. "Yip" Harburg
Music by Vernon Duke

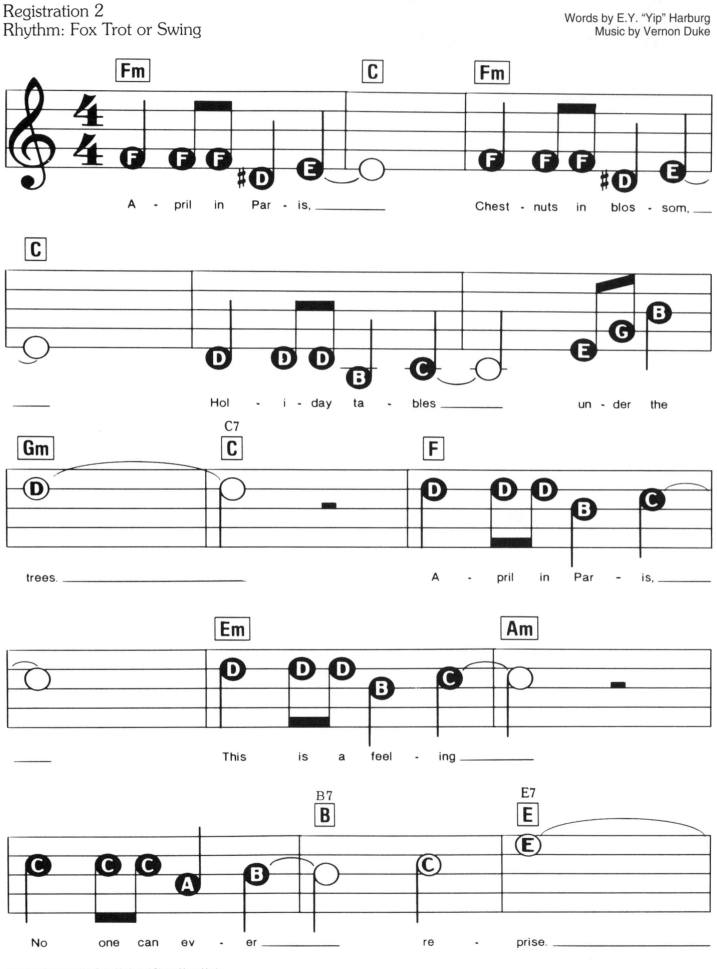

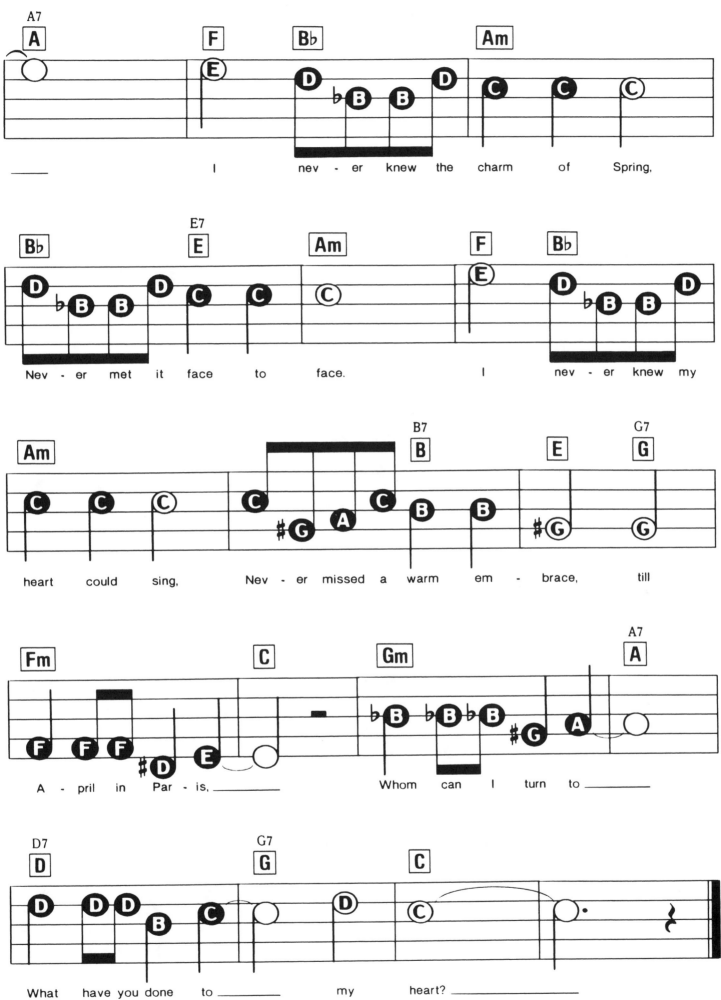

Autumn Leaves

Registration 2
Rhythm: Fox Trot or Swing

English lyric by Johnny Mercer
French lyric by Jacques Prevert
Music by Joseph Kosma

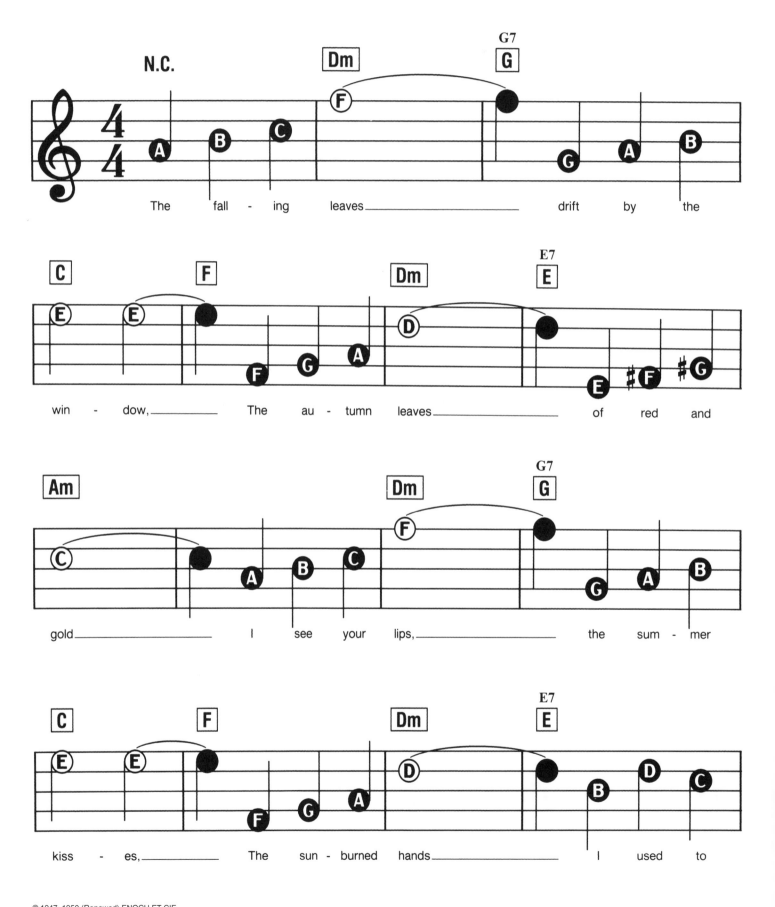

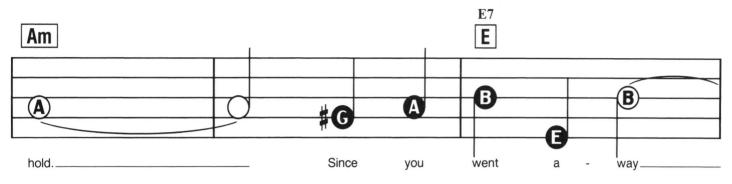

hold._____ Since you went a - way_____

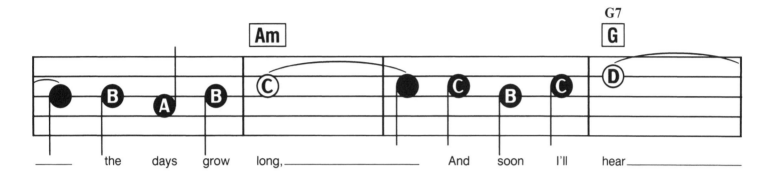

_____ the days grow long,_____ And soon I'll hear_____

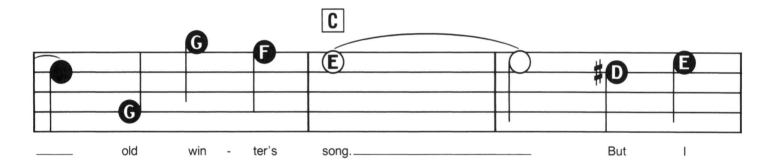

_____ old win - ter's song._____ But I

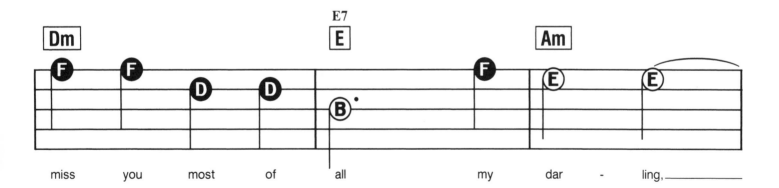

miss you most of all my dar - ling,_____

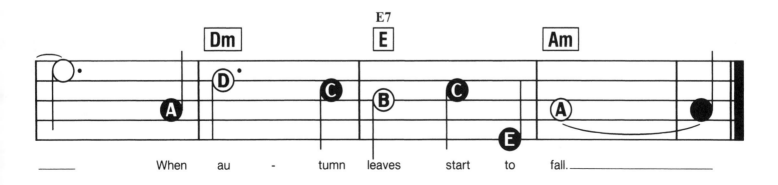

_____ When au - tumn leaves start to fall._____

Beyond the Sea

Registration 7
Rhythm: Slow Ballad or Rock

By Albert Lasry and Charles Trenet
English Lyrics by Jack Lawrence

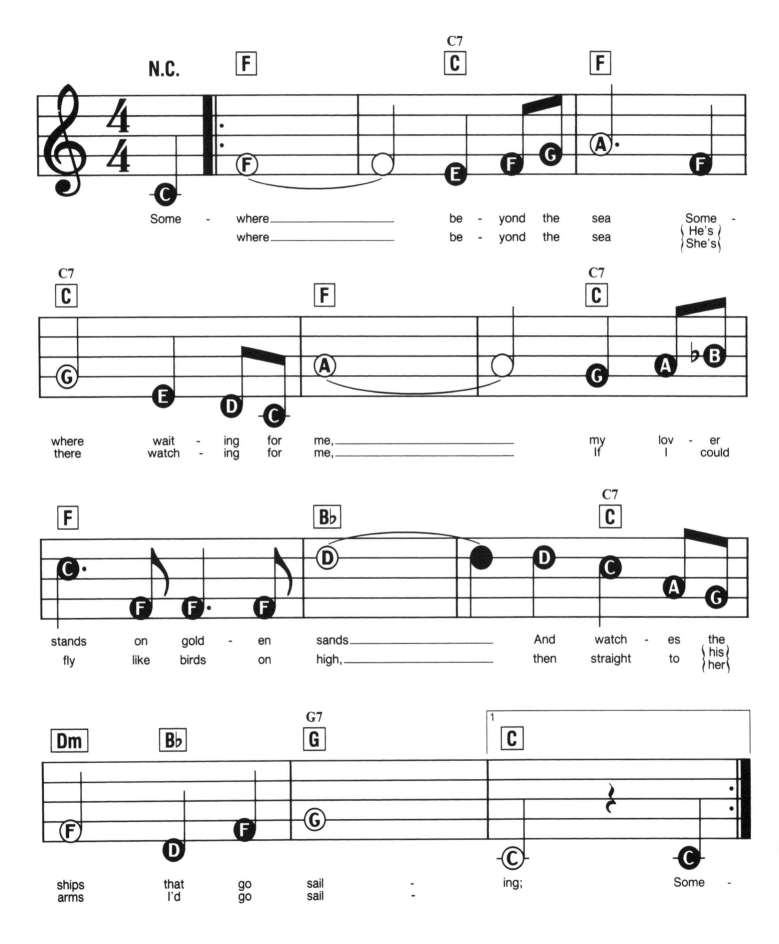

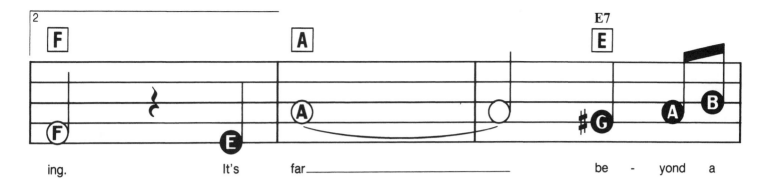

ing.   It's   far_____   be - yond a

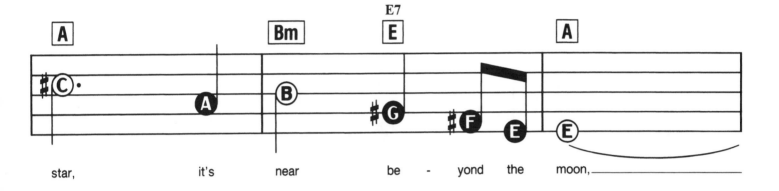

star,   it's   near   be - yond the moon,_____

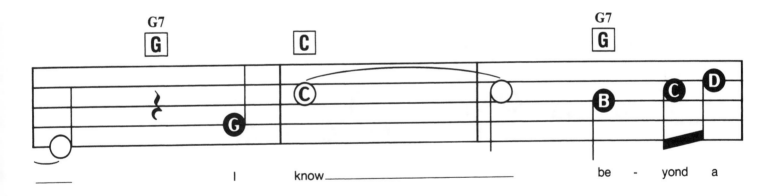

_____   I   know_____   be - yond a

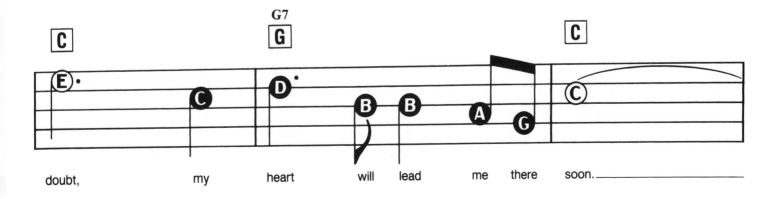

doubt,   my   heart   will   lead   me   there   soon._____

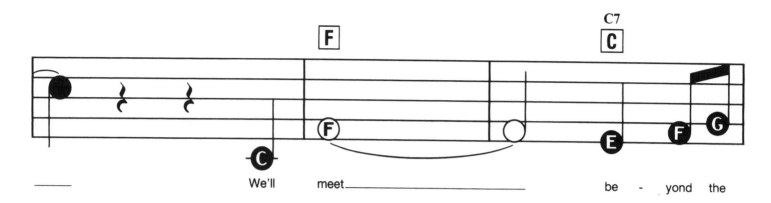

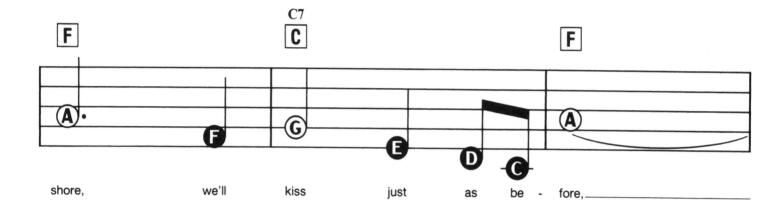

We'll meet _____ be - yond the

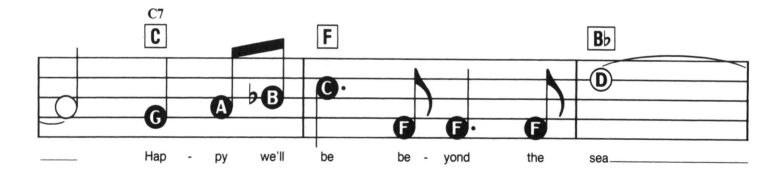

shore, we'll kiss just as be - fore, _____

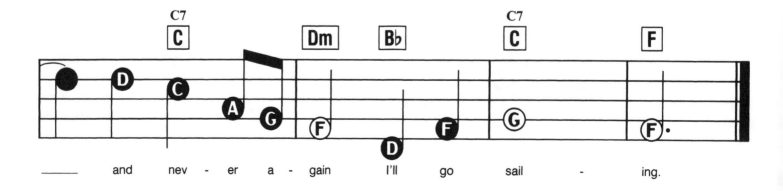

____ Hap - py we'll be be - yond the sea _____

and nev - er a - gain I'll go sail - ing.

Bring Him Home
from LES MISÉRABLES

Registration 1
Rhythm: Ballad

Music by Claude-Michel Schönberg
Lyrics by Alain Boublil and Herbert Kretzmer

God on high, _____ hear my prayer. _____
peace, _____ bring him joy. _____

_____ In my need _____ You have
He is young, he is

al - ways been there. He is young, _____
on - ly a boy. You can take, _____

_____ he's a - fraid. Let him rest, _____
You can give. Let him be, _____

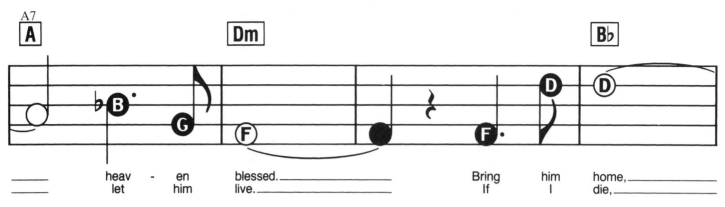

heav - en blessed. Bring him home,
let him live. If I die,

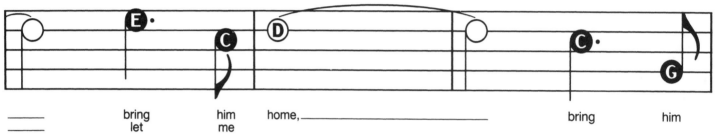

bring him home,
let me

bring him

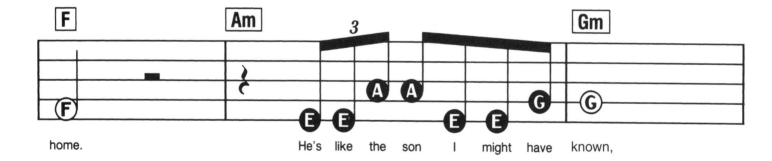

home. He's like the son I might have known,

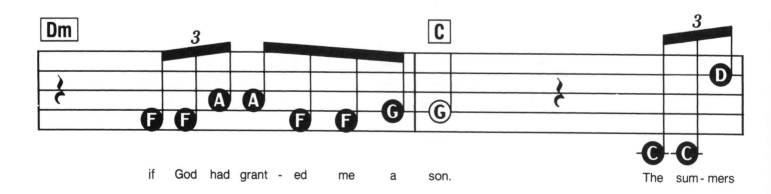

if God had grant - ed me a son. The sum - mers

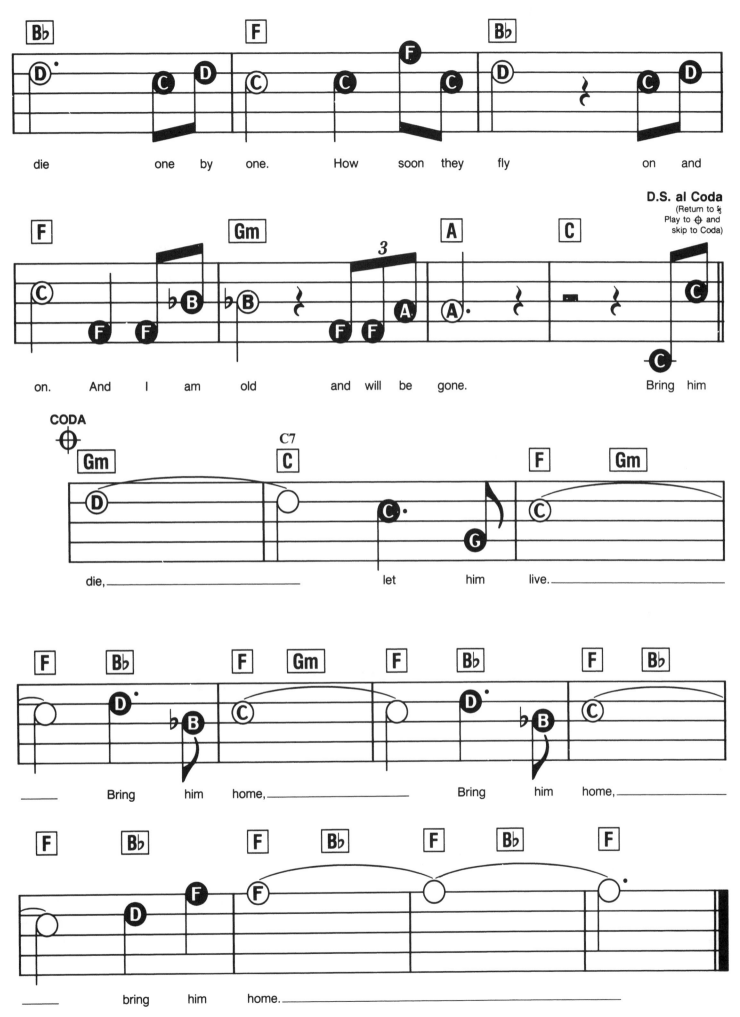

C'est Magnifique
from CAN-CAN

Registration 5
Rhythm: Fox Trot or Swing

Words and Music by
Cole Porter

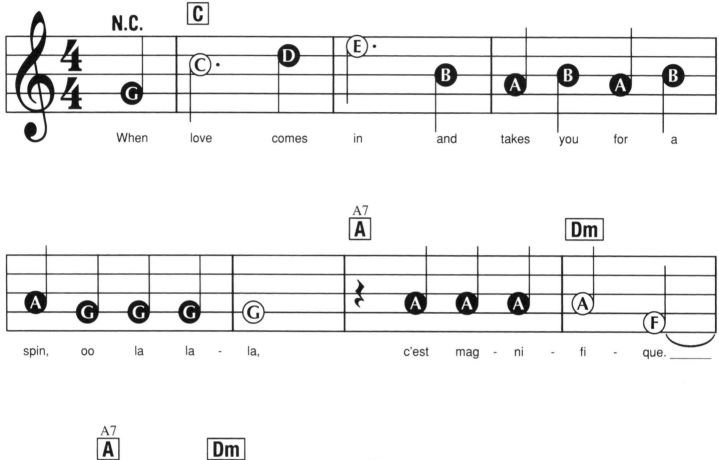

When love comes in and takes you for a

spin, oo la la - la, c'est mag - ni - fi - que. _____

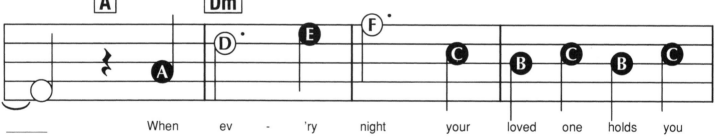

_____ When ev - 'ry night your loved one holds you

tight, oo la la - la, c'est mag - ni -

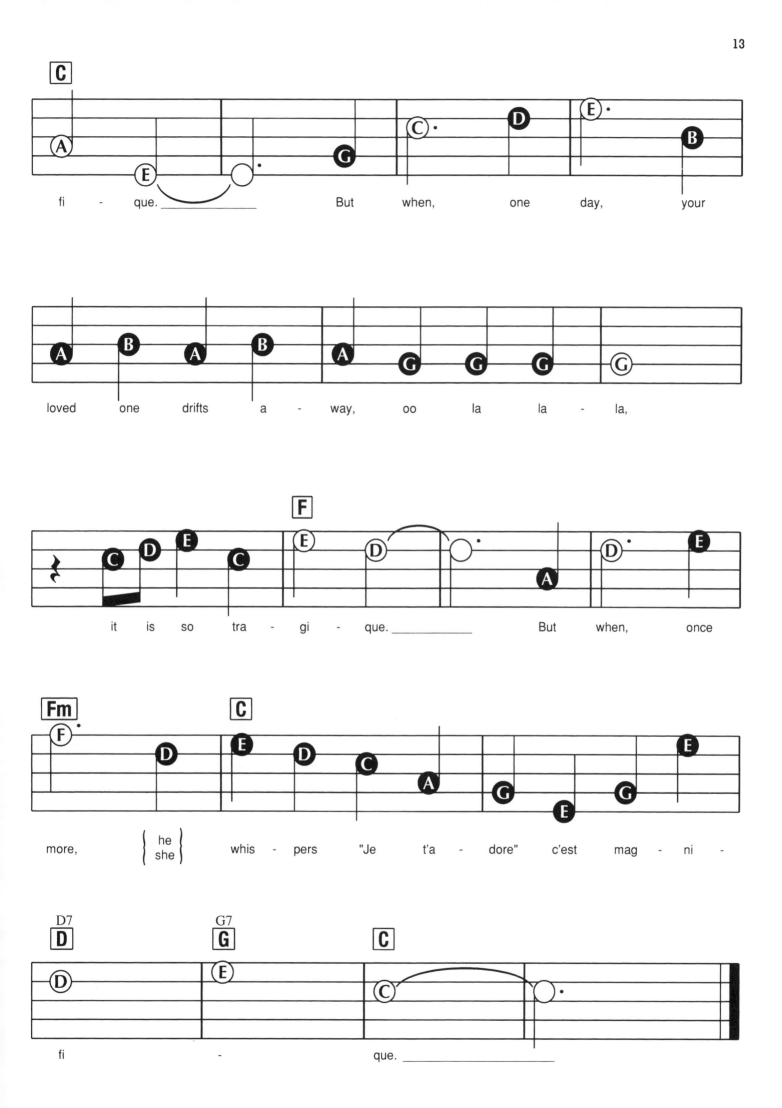

I Love Paris
from CAN-CAN
from HIGH SOCIETY

Registration 9
Rhythm: Fox Trot

Words and Music by
Cole Porter

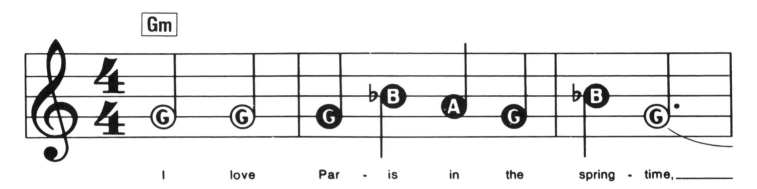

I love Par - is in the spring - time,_____

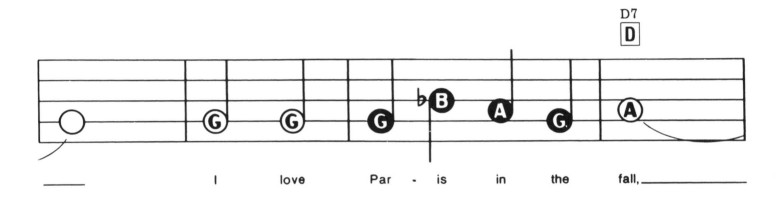

_____ I love Par - is in the fall,_____

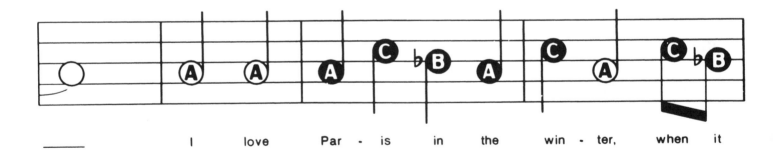

_____ I love Par - is in the win - ter, when it

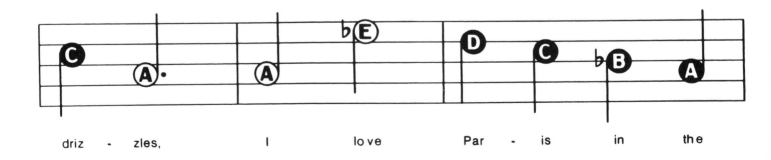

driz - zles, I love Par - is in the

15

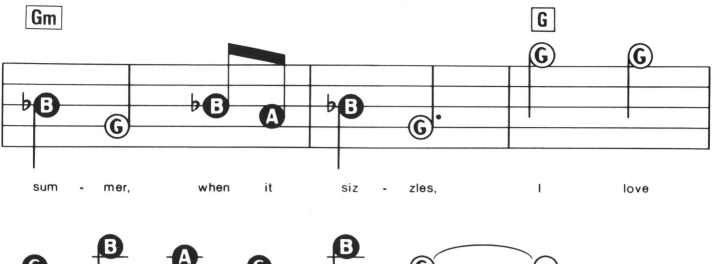

sum - mer, when it siz - zles, I love

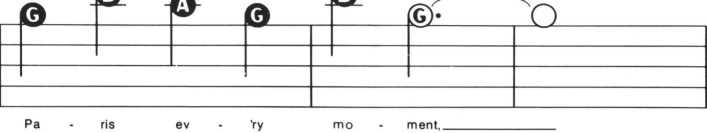

Pa - ris ev - 'ry mo - ment,_____

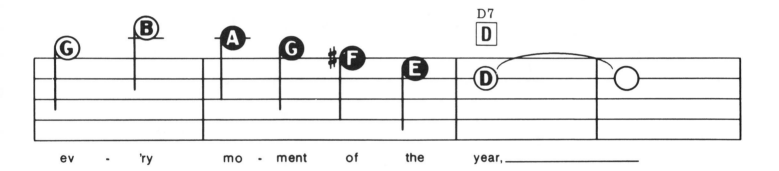

ev - 'ry mo - ment of the year,_____

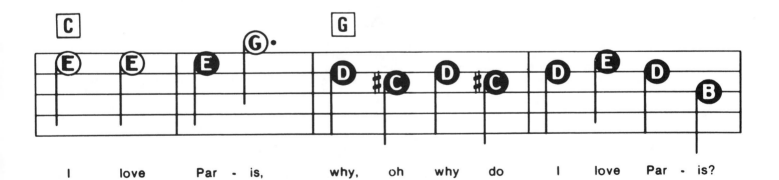

I love Par - is, why, oh why do I love Par - is?

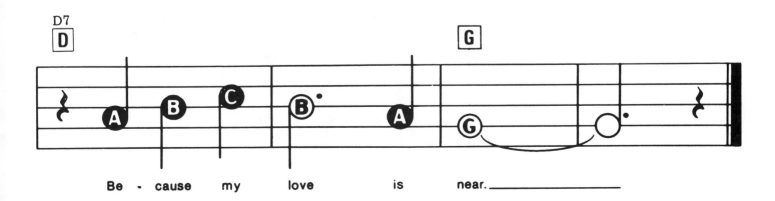

Be - cause my love is near._____

I Will Wait for You
from THE UMBRELLAS OF CHERBOURG

Registration 9
Rhythm: Fox Trot or Swing

Music by Michel Legrand
Original French Text by Jacques Demy
English Words by Norman Gimbel

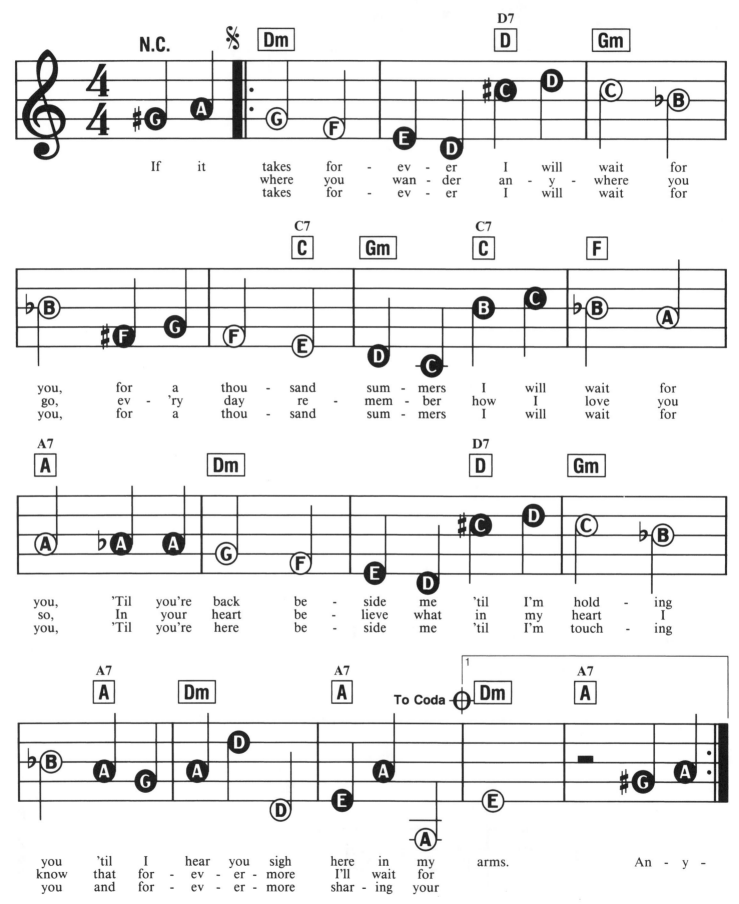

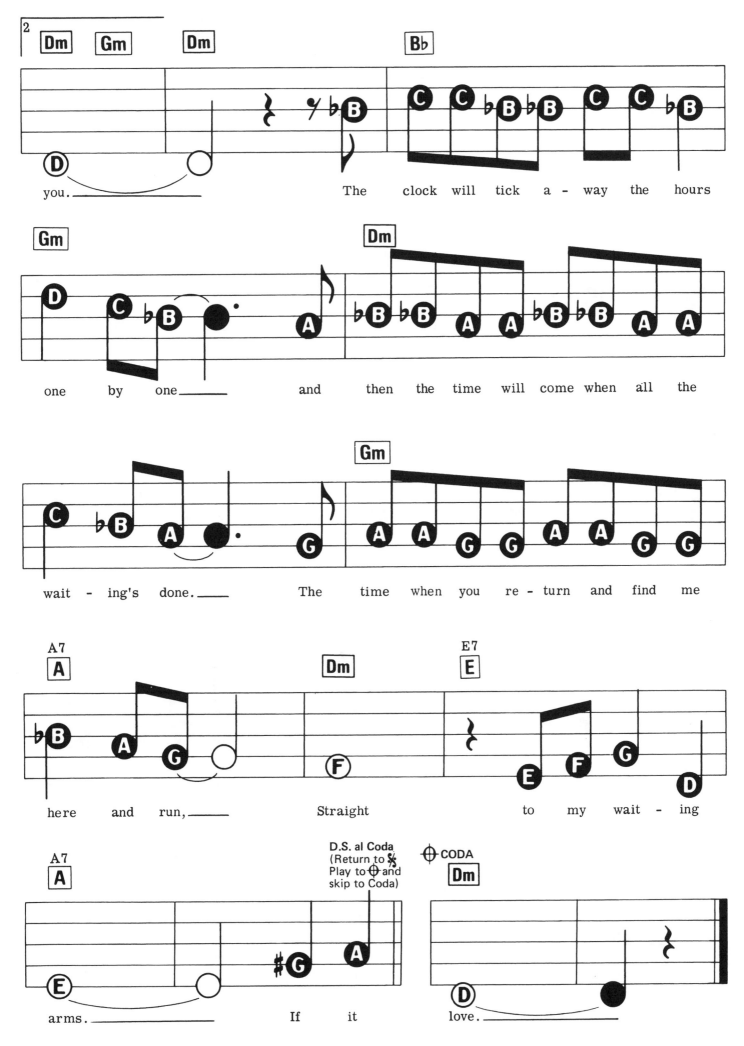

If We Only Have Love
(Quand on n'a que l'amour)
from JACQUES BREL IS ALIVE AND WELL AND LIVING IN PARIS

Registration 4
Rhythm: Ballad

French Words and Music by Jacques Brel
English Words by Mort Shuman and Eric Blau

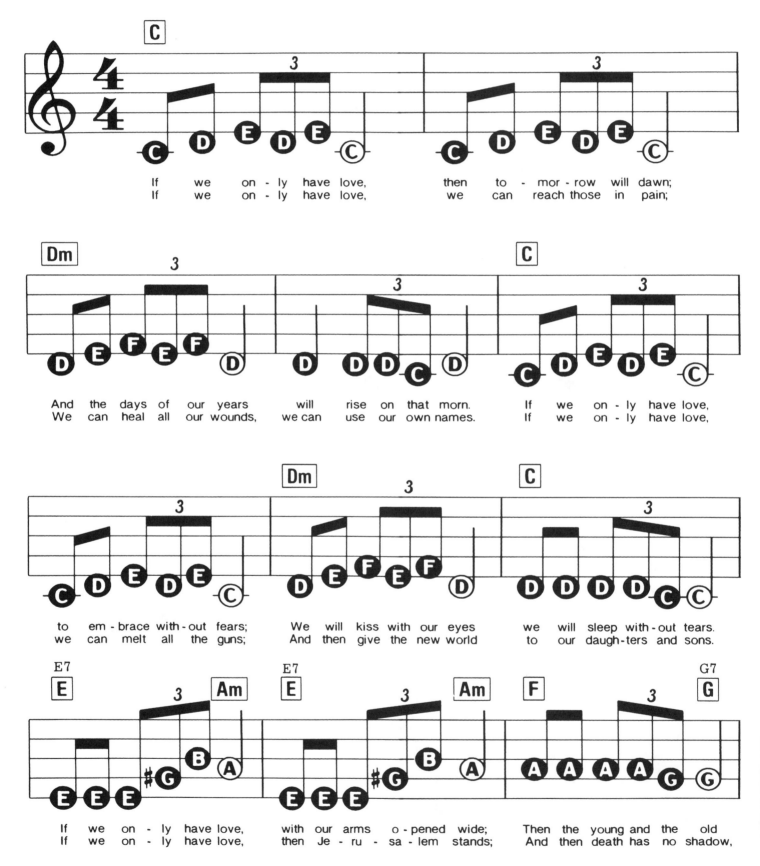

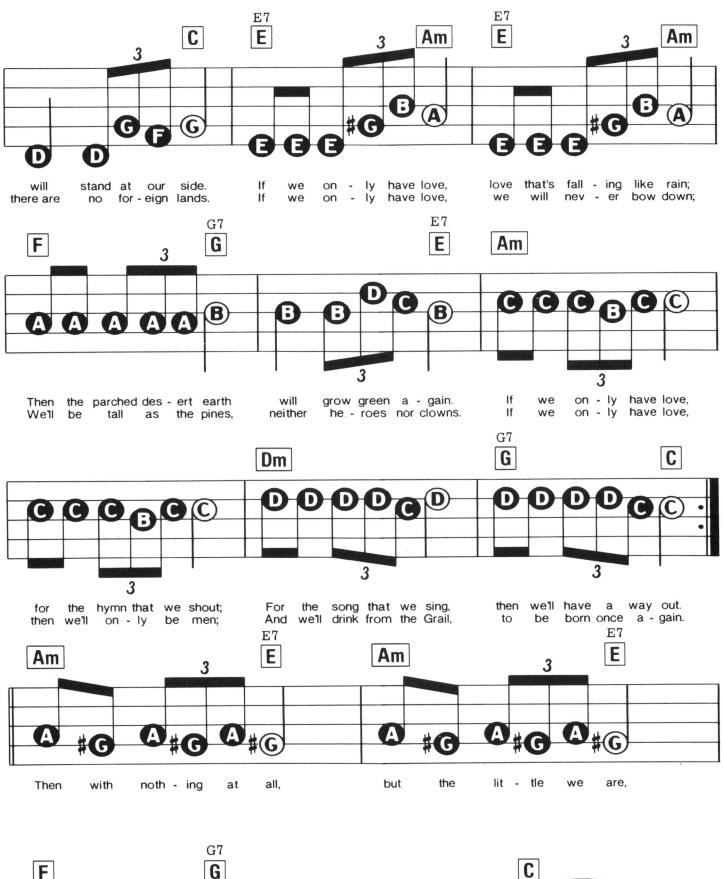

will   stand at our side.   If   we   on - ly have love,   love that's fall - ing like rain;
there are   no for - eign lands.   If   we   on - ly have love,   we   will nev - er bow down;

Then   the parched des - ert earth   will   grow green a - gain.   If   we   on - ly have love,
We'll be   tall   as   the pines,   neither   he - roes nor clowns.   If   we   on - ly have love,

for   the hymn that we shout;   For   the song that we sing,   then   we'll have a   way out.
then   we'll on - ly be men;   And   we'll drink from the Grail,   to   be born once a - gain.

Then   with   noth - ing   at   all,   but   the   lit - tle   we   are,

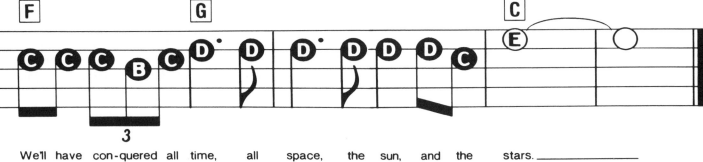

We'll have con - quered all time,   all   space,   the sun, and the   stars. _____

If You Go Away

Registration 10
Rhythm: Waltz or Jazz Waltz

French Words and Music by Jacques Brel
English Words by Rod McKuen

21

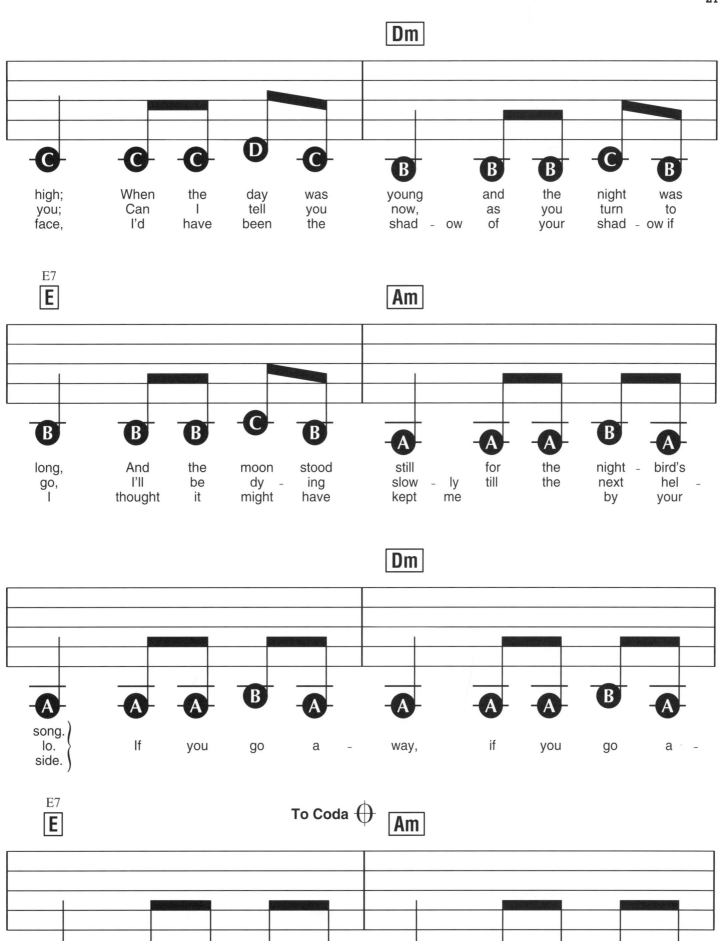

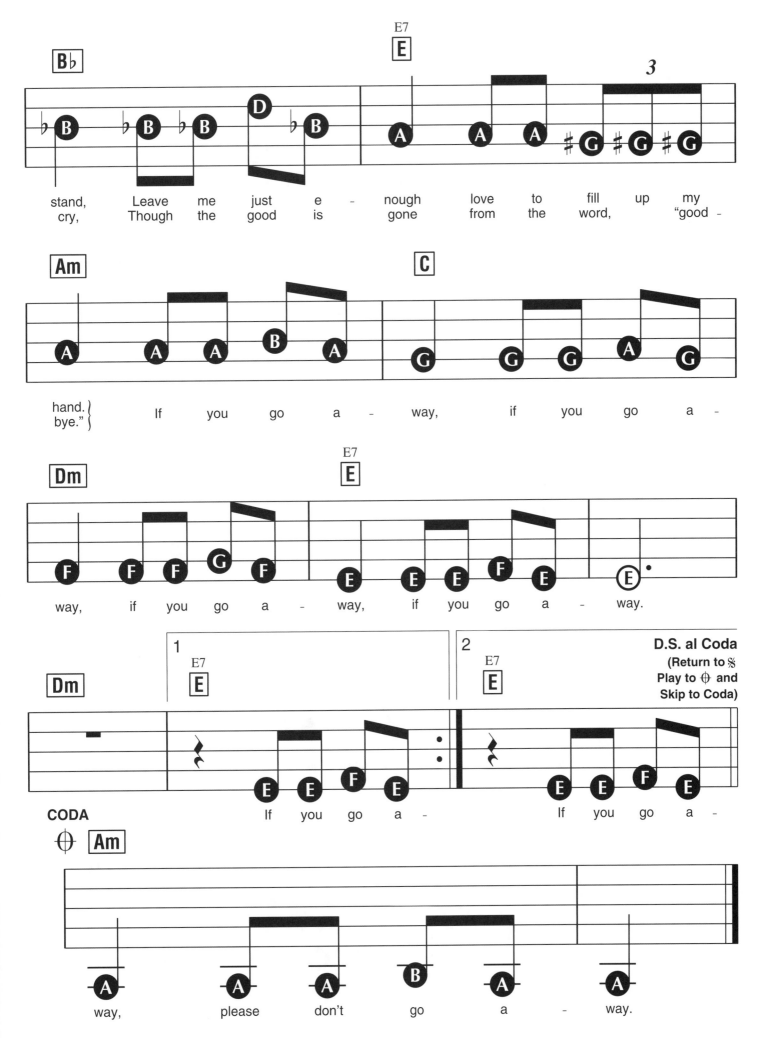

La Marseillaise

Registration 4
Rhythm: March

Words and Music by
Claude Rouget de Lisle

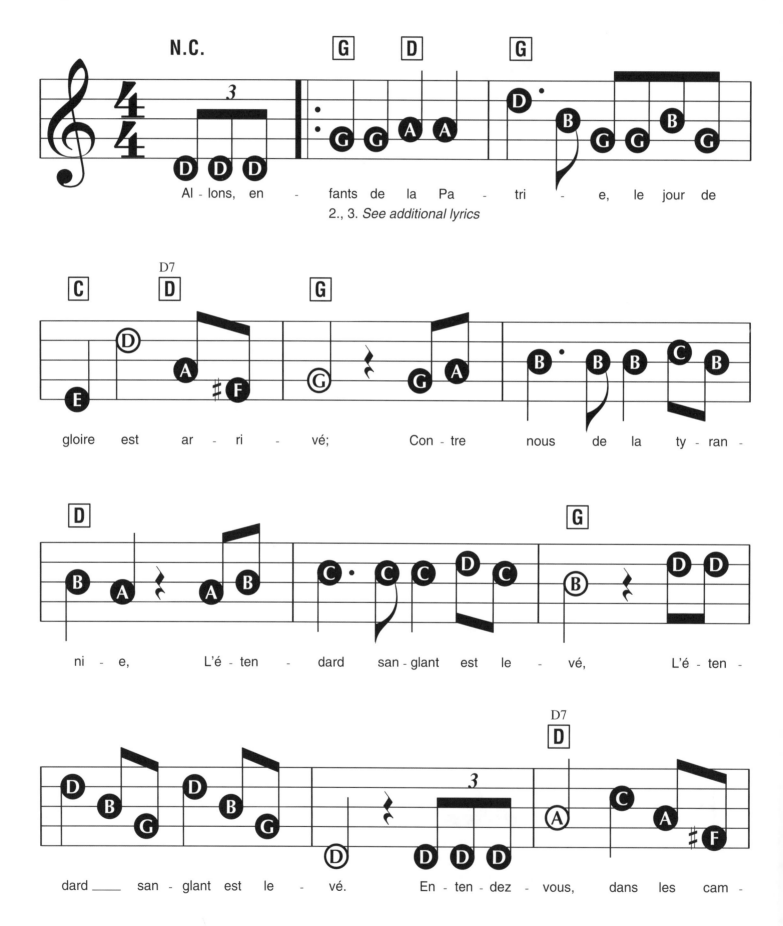

Al - lons, en - fants de la Pa - tri - e, le jour de

2., 3. *See additional lyrics*

gloire est ar - ri - vé; Con - tre nous de la ty - ran -

ni - e, L'é - ten - dard san - glant est le - vé, L'é - ten -

dard ___ san - glant est le - vé. En - ten - dez - vous, dans les cam -

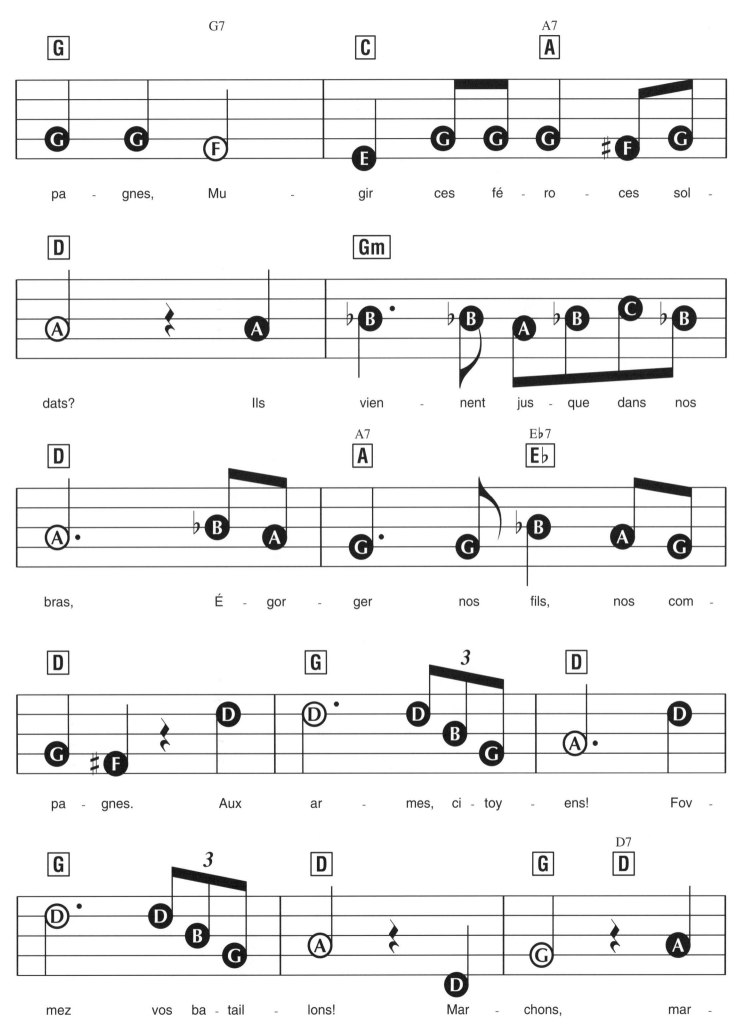

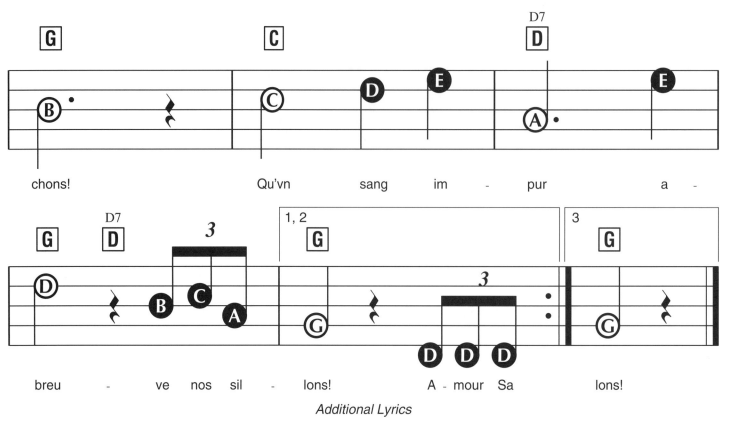

chons!   Qu'vn   sang   im - pur   a -

breu - ve   nos   sil - lons!   A - mour Sa   lons!

Additional Lyrics

2. Amour Sacré de la Patrie,
   Conduis, soutiens, nos bras vengeurs.
   Liberté, liberté chérie
   Combats avec tes défenseurs!
   Combats avec tes défenseurs!
   Sous nos drapeaux, que la victoire
   Accours à tes mâles accents!
   Que tes ennemis expirants
   Voient ton triomphe et notre gloire.
      Aux armes, *etc.*

3. Nous entrerons dans la carrière
   Quand nos aînés n'y seront plus.
   Nous y trouverons leur poussière
   Et la trace de leurs vertus,
   Et la trace de leurs vertus,
   Bein moins jaloux de leur survivre
   Que de partager leur cercueil
   Nous aurons le sublime orgueil
   De les venger ou de les suivre.
      Aux armes, *etc.*

English Translation

1. Arise you children of our Motherland,
   Oh now is here our glorious day!
   Over us the bloodstained banner
   Of tyranny holds sway!
   Of tyranny holds sway!
   Oh, do you hear there in our fields
   The roar of those fierce fighting men?
   Who came right here into our midst
   To slaughter sons, wives and kin.
      To arms, oh citizens!
      Form up in serried ranks!
      March on, march on!
      And drench our fields
      With their tainted blood!

2. Supreme devotion to our Motherland,
   Guides and sustains avenging hands.
   Liberty, oh dearest Liberty,
   Come fight with your shielding bands!
   Come fight with your shielding bands.
   Beneath our banner come, oh Victory,
   Run at your soul-stirring cry.
   Oh come, come see your foes now die,
   Witness your pride and our glory.
      To arms, *etc.*

3. Into the fight we too shall enter,
   When our fathers are dead and gone,
   We shall find their bones laid down to rest,
   With the fame of their glories won,
   With the fame of their glories won!
   Oh, to survive them care we not,
   Glad are we to share their grave,
   Great honor is to be our lot
   To follow or to venge our brave.
      To arms, *etc.*

A Man and a Woman
(Un homme et une femme)
from A MAN AND A WOMAN

Original Words by Pierre Barouh
English Words by Jerry Keller
Music by Francis Lai

Registration 5
Rhythm: Fox Trot

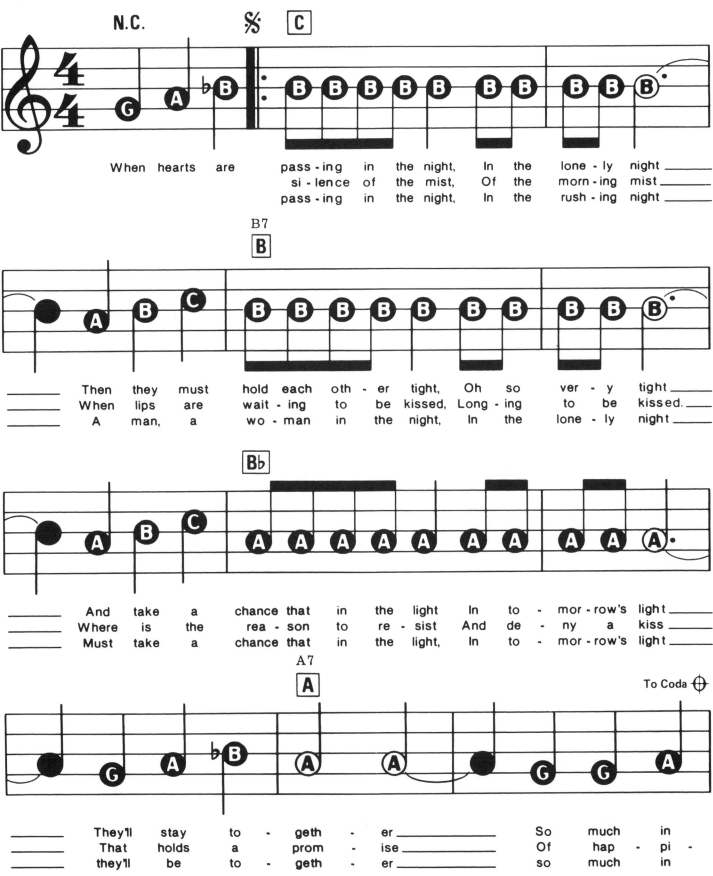

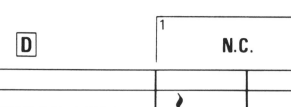

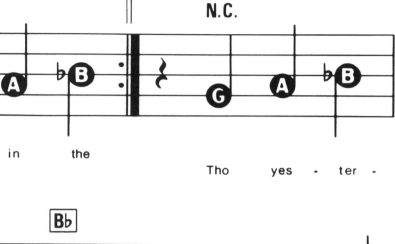

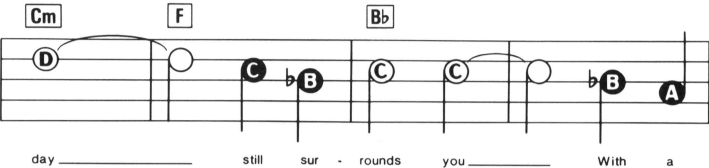

love.

ness.

And in the

Tho yes - ter -

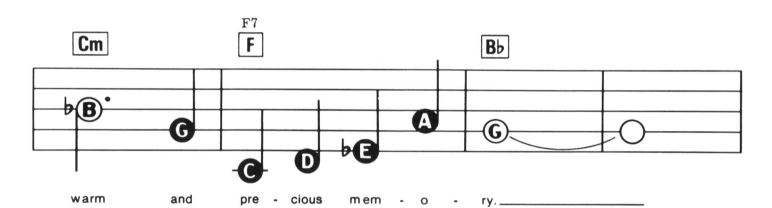

day _____ still sur - rounds you _____ With a

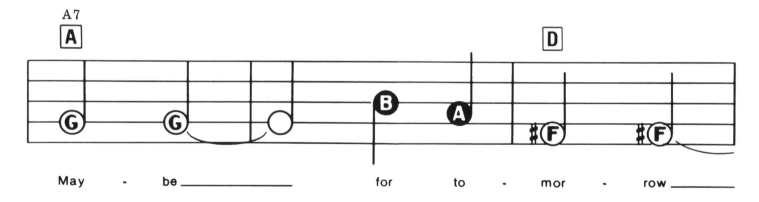

warm and pre - cious mem - o - ry. _____

A7

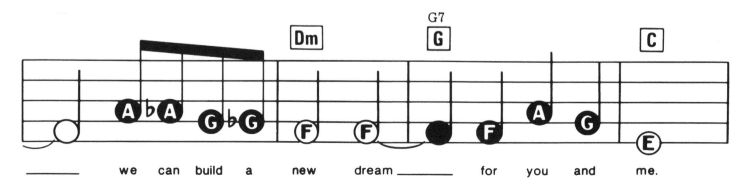

May - be _____ for to - mor - row _____

we can build a new dream _____ for you and me.

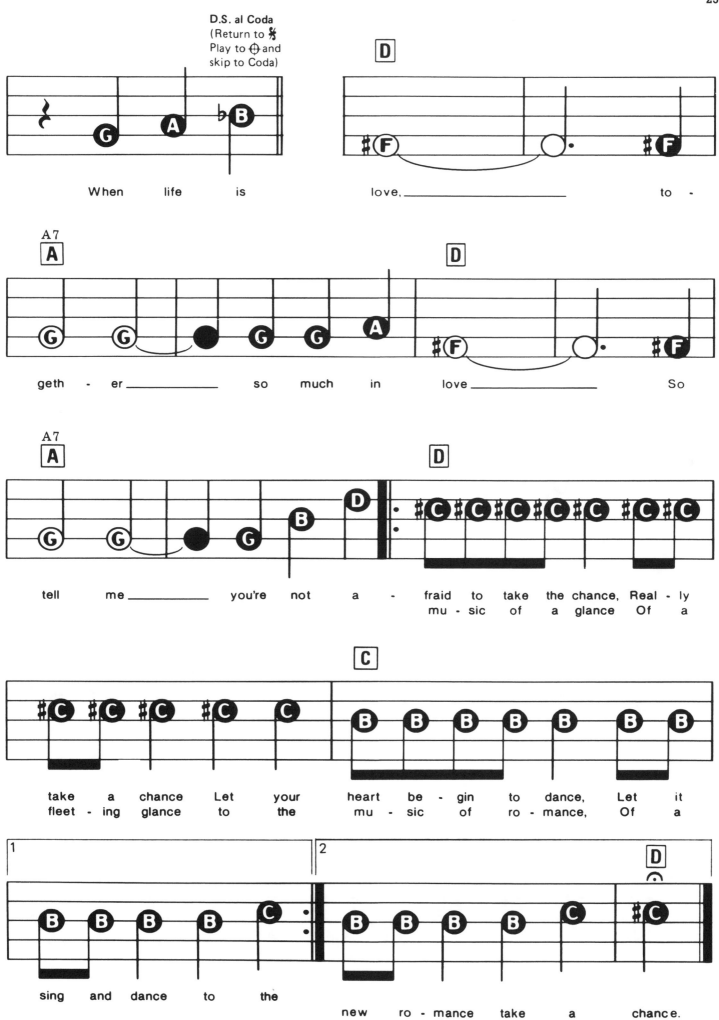

Let It Be Me
(Je t'appartiens)

Registration 8
Rhythm: Rock

English Words by Mann Curtis
French Words by Pierre DeLanoe
Music by Gilbert Becaud

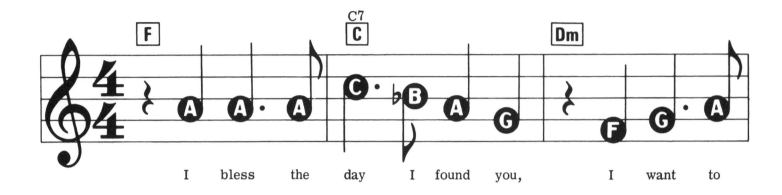

I bless the day I found you, I want to

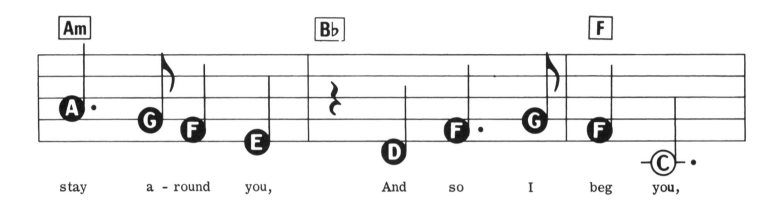

stay a - round you, And so I beg you,

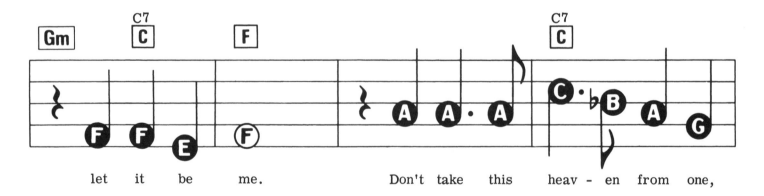

let it be me. Don't take this heav - en from one,

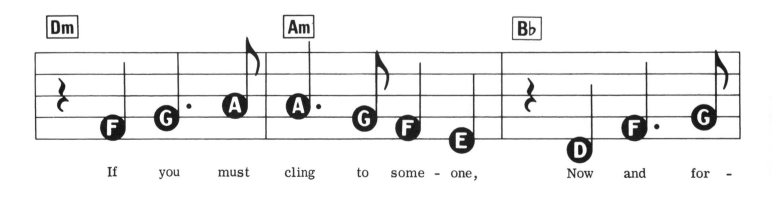

If you must cling to some - one, Now and for -

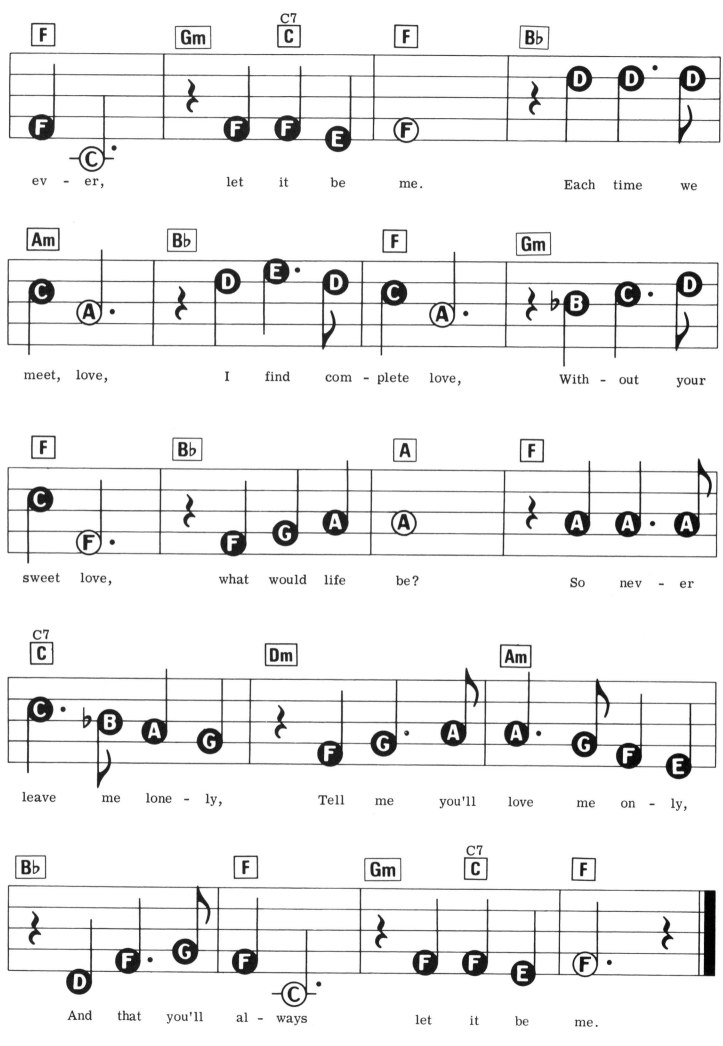

Michelle

Registration 1
Rhythm: Rock

Words and Music by John Lennon
and Paul McCartney

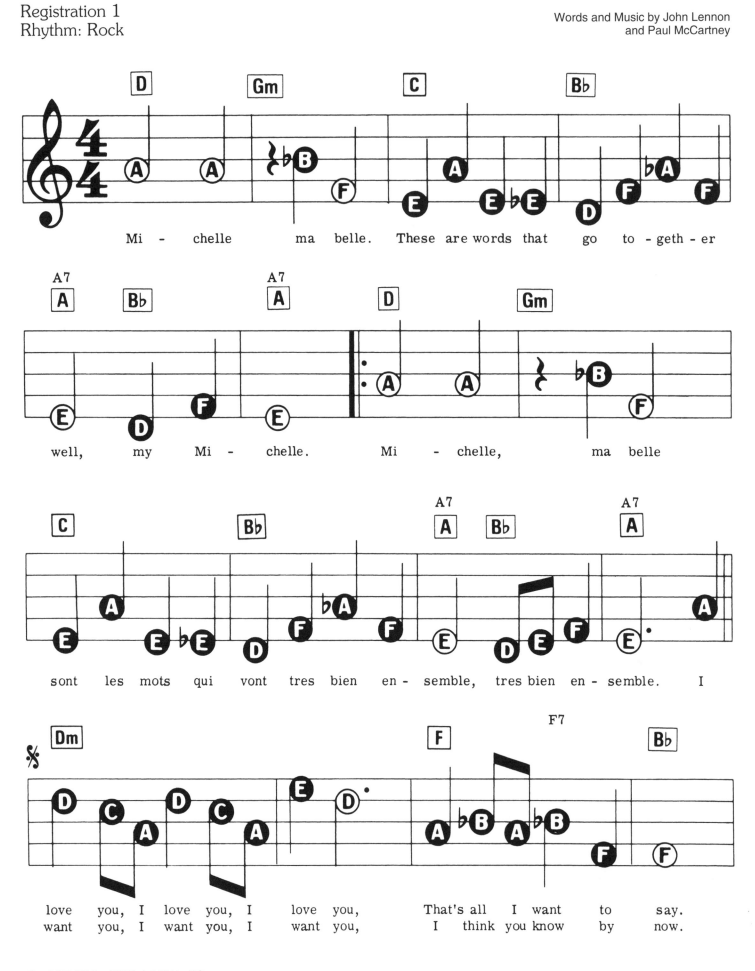

Milord

Registration 3
Rhythm: Fox Trot

Lyric by Georges Moustaki
Music by Marguerite Monnot

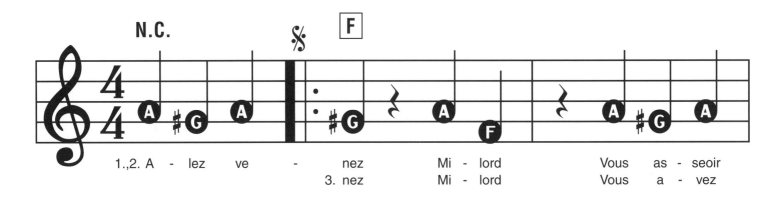

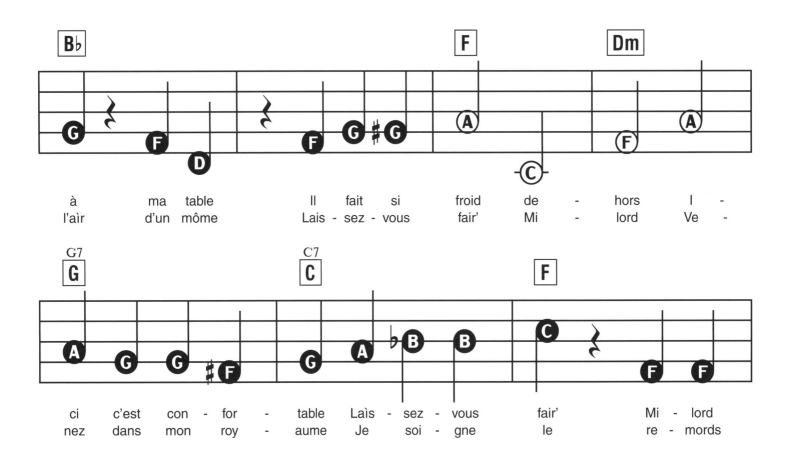

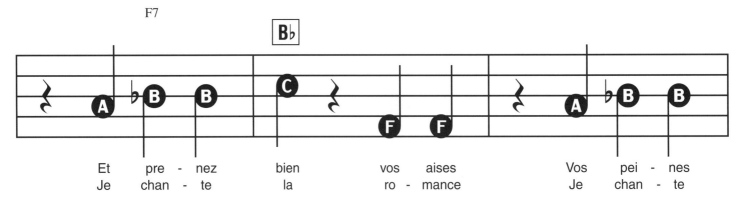

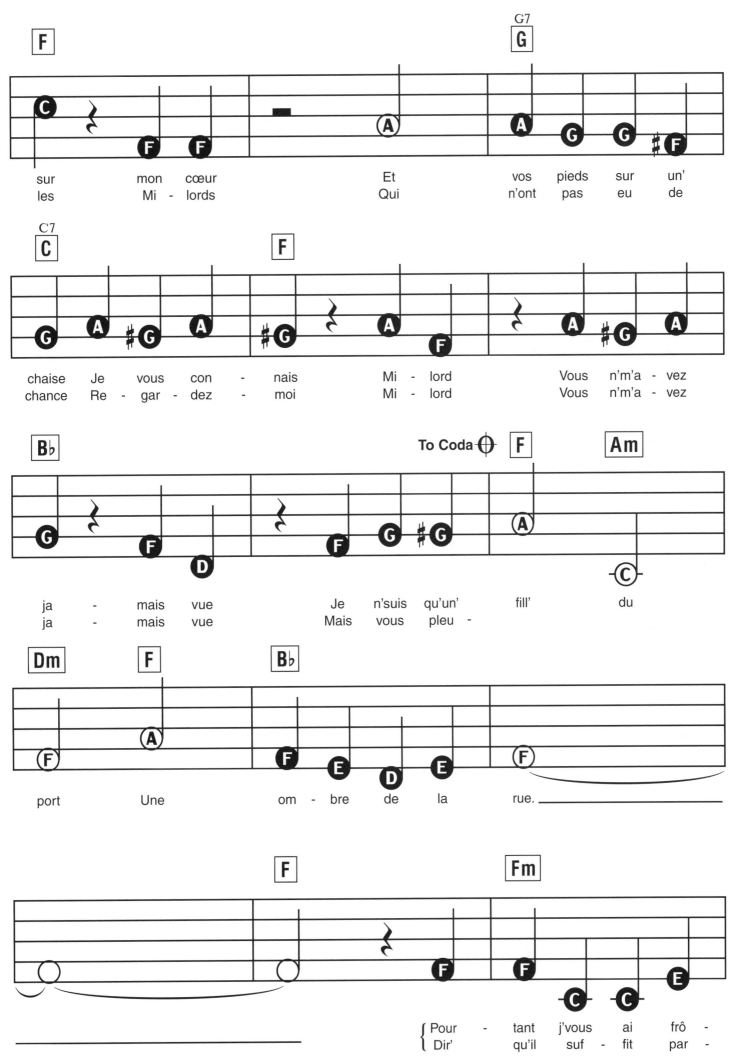

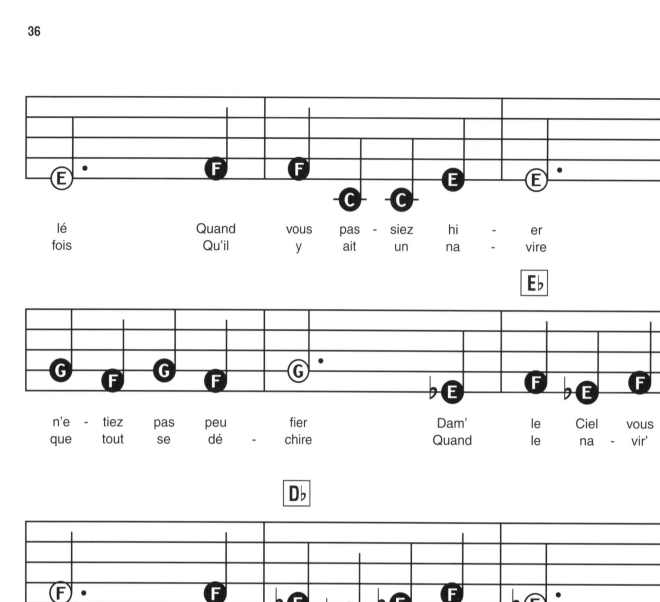

lé   Quand   vous   pas - siez   hi - er   Vous
fois   Qu'il   y   ait   un   na - vire   Pour

E♭

n'e - tiez   pas   peu   fier   Dam'   le   Ciel   vous com -
que   tout   se   dé - chire   Quand   le   na - vir'   s'en

D♭

blait   Vo - tre   fou - lard   de   soie   Flot -
va   Il   emm' - nait   a - vec   lui   La

tant   sur   vos   é - paules   Vous   a - viez   le   beau
douce   aux   vos   yeux   si   tendres   Qui   n'a   pas   su   com -

B♭m

rôle   On   au - rait   dit   le   roi   Vous
prendre   Qu'ell'   bri - sait   vo - tre   vie   L'a -

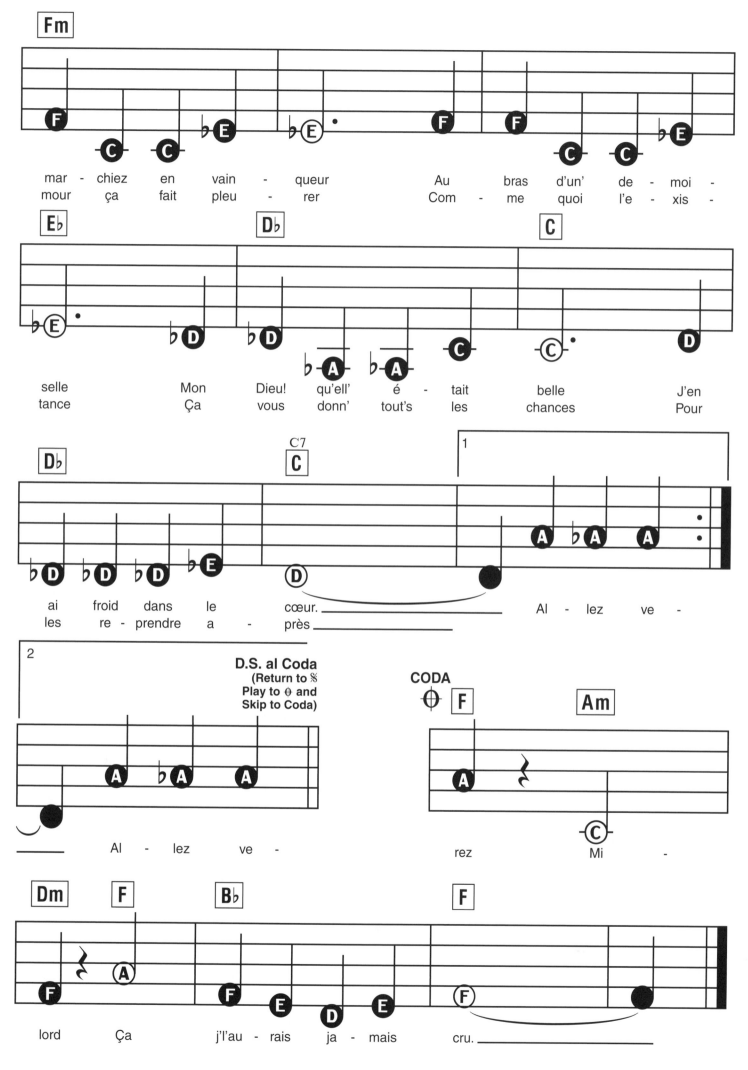

Non, je ne regrette rien

Registration 8
Rhythm: Slow Rock

Music by Charles Dumont
French Lyric by Michel Vaucaire

Non! _____ Rien de rien, _____

Non! _____ Je ne re - grette ri - en. _____

_____ Ni le bien, _____ qu'on m'a

fait, _____ ni le mal _____

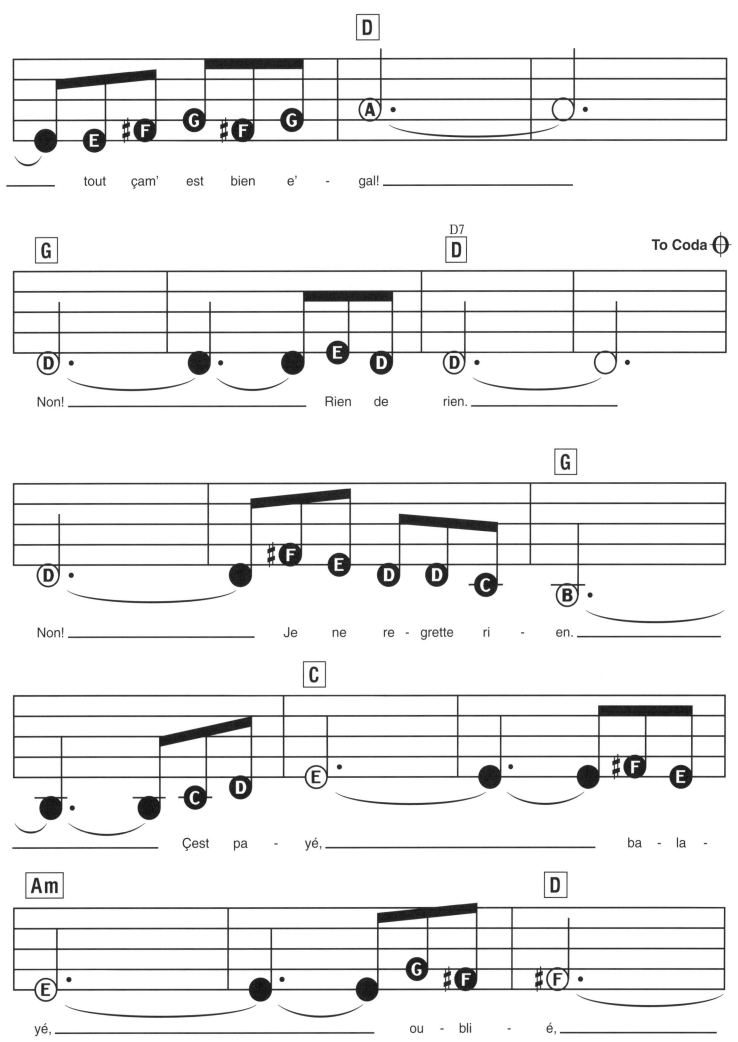

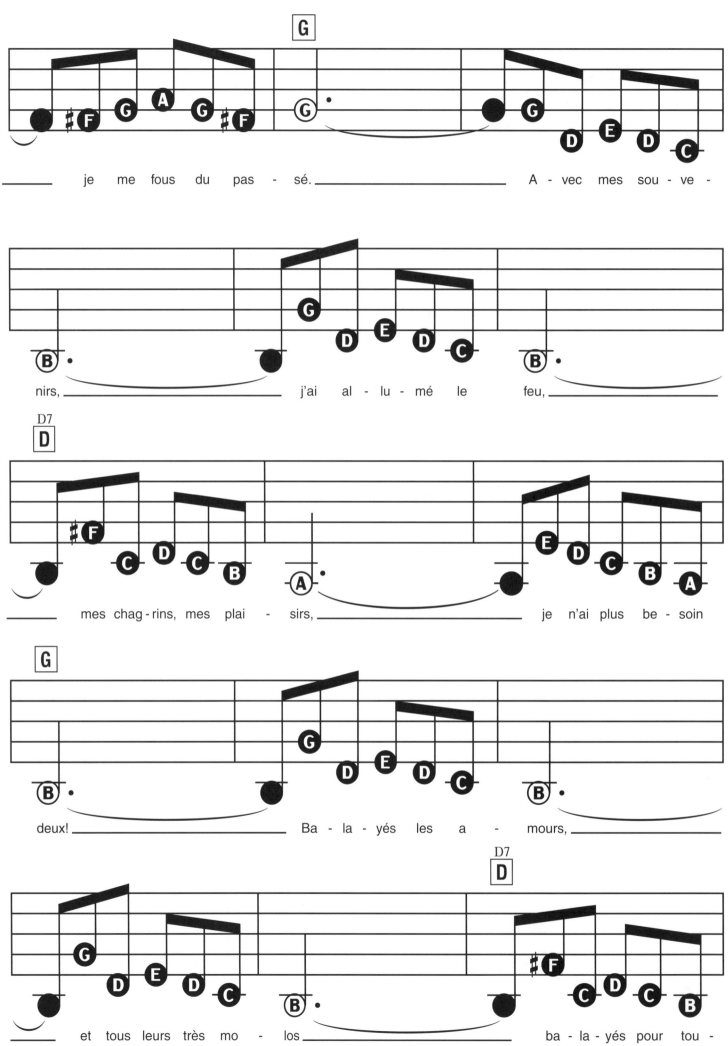

D.C. al Coda
(Return to beginning
Play to ⊕ and
Skip to Coda)

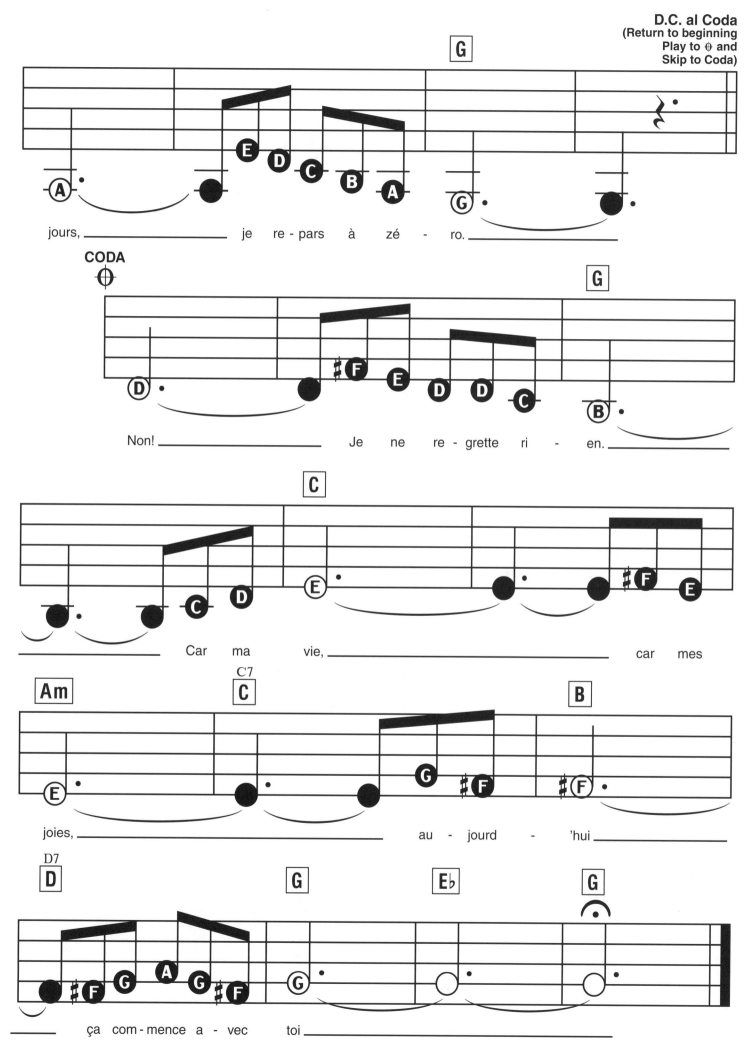

On My Own
from LES MISÉRABLES

Music by Claude-Michel Schönberg
Lyrics by Alain Boublil, John Caird, Trevor Nunn,
Jean-Marc Natel and Herbert Kretzmer

Registration 1
Rhythm: Ballad

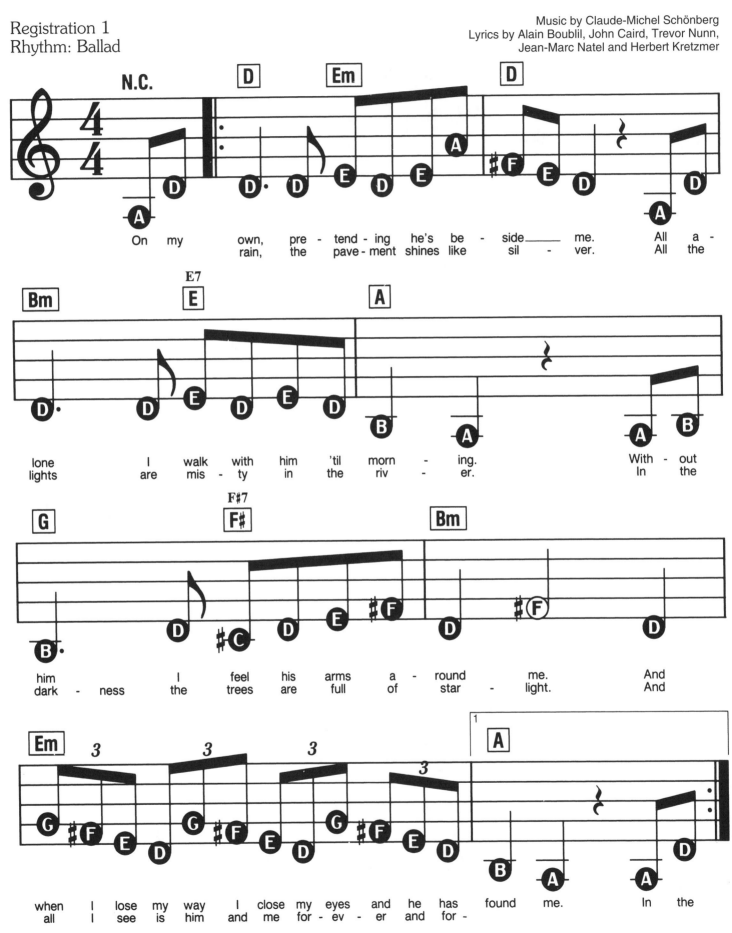

On my own, pre- tend- ing he's be- side me. All a-
rain, the pave- ment shines like sil- ver. All the

lone I walk with him 'til morn- ing. With- out
lights are mis- ty in the riv- er. In the

him I feel his arms a- round me. And
dark- ness the trees are full of star- light. And

when I lose my way I close my eyes and he has found me. In the
all I see is him and me for- ev- er and for-

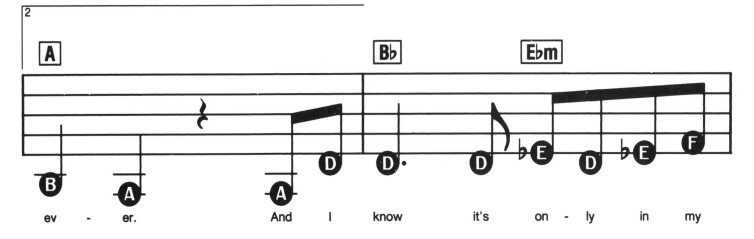

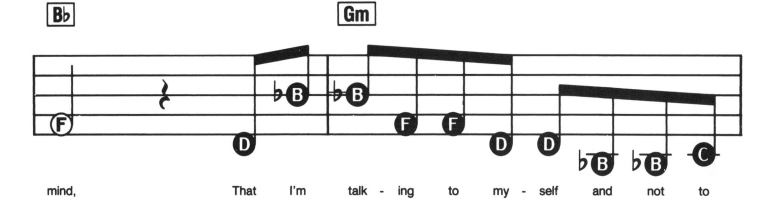

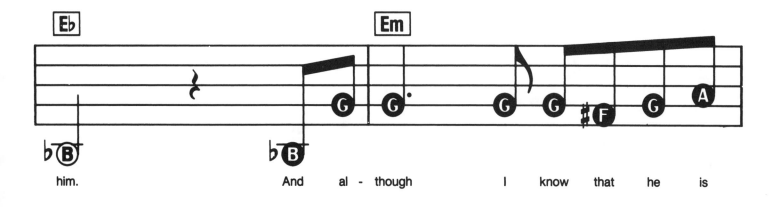

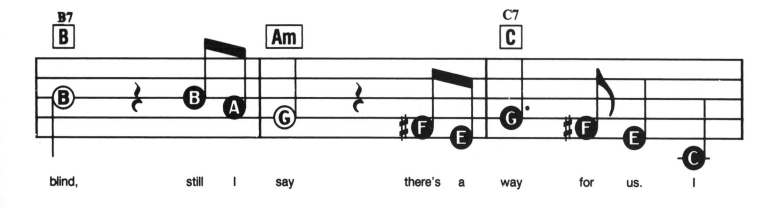

43

44

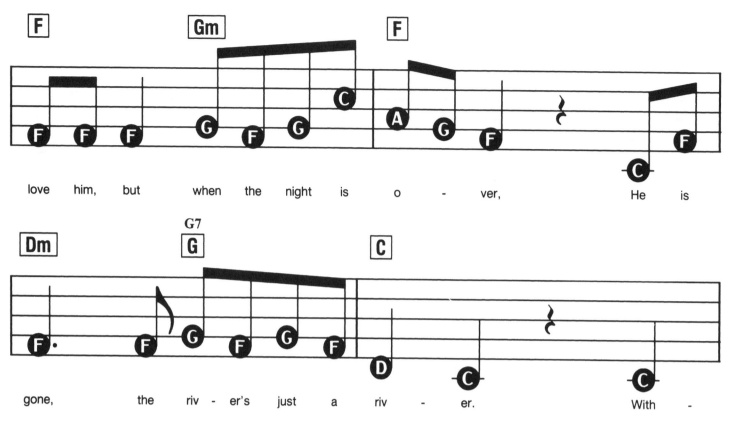

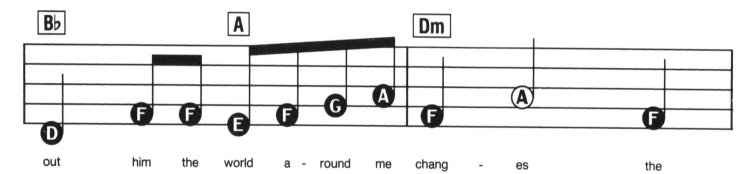

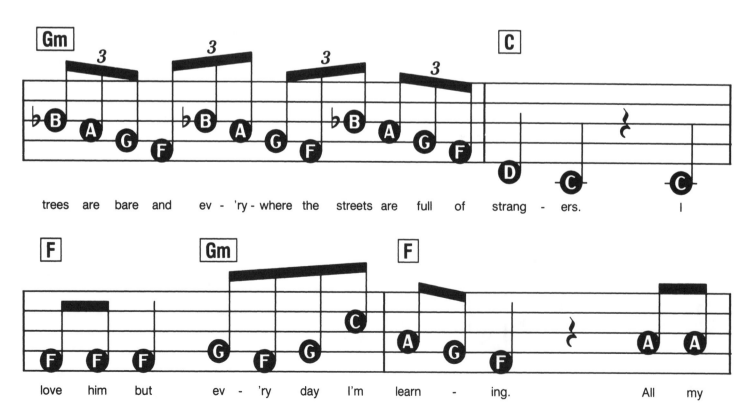

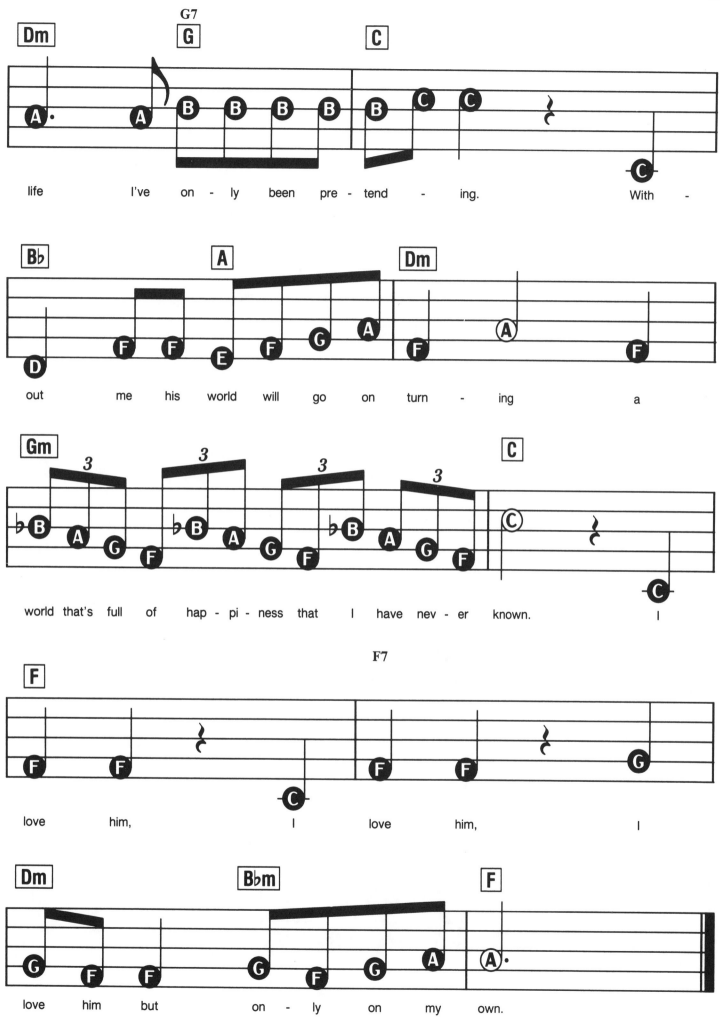

The Petite Waltz

Registration 5
Rhythm: Waltz

English Lyric by E.A. Ellington and Phyllis Claire
Music by Joe Heyne

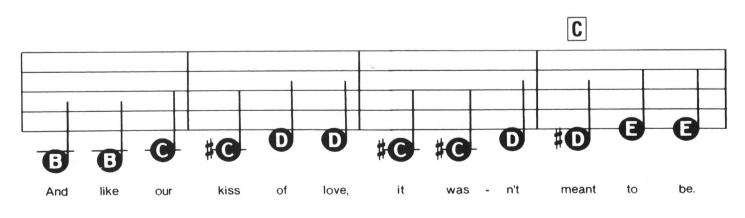

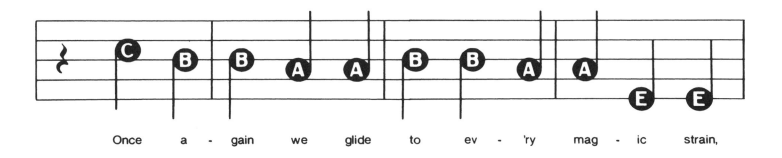

Once a - gain we glide to ev - 'ry mag - ic strain,

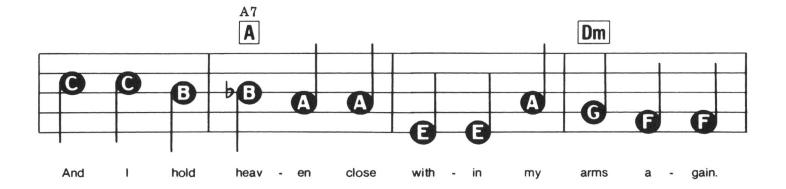

And I hold heav - en close with - in my arms a - gain.

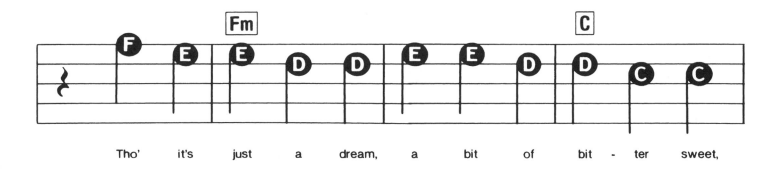

Tho' it's just a dream, a bit of bit - ter sweet,

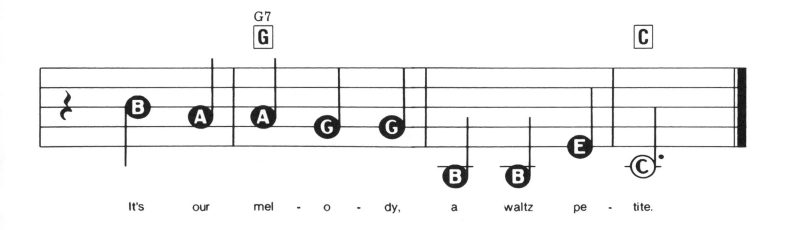

It's our mel - o - dy, a waltz pe - tite.

Pigalle

English Lyric by Charles Newman
French Lyric by Geo Koger, Georges Ulmer and Guy Luypaerts
Music by Georges Ulmer and Guy Luypaerts

Registration 5
Rhythm: Waltz

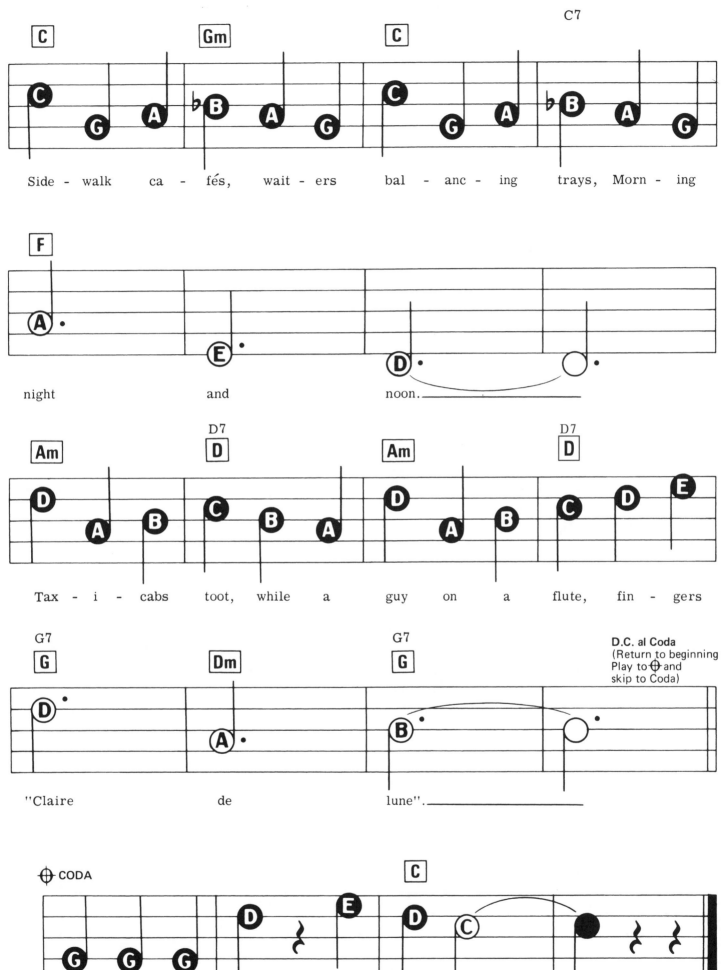

The Poor People of Paris
(Jean's Song)

Original French words by Rene Rouzaud
English words by Jack Lawrence
Music by Marguerite Monnot

Registration 4
Rhythm: Fox Trot

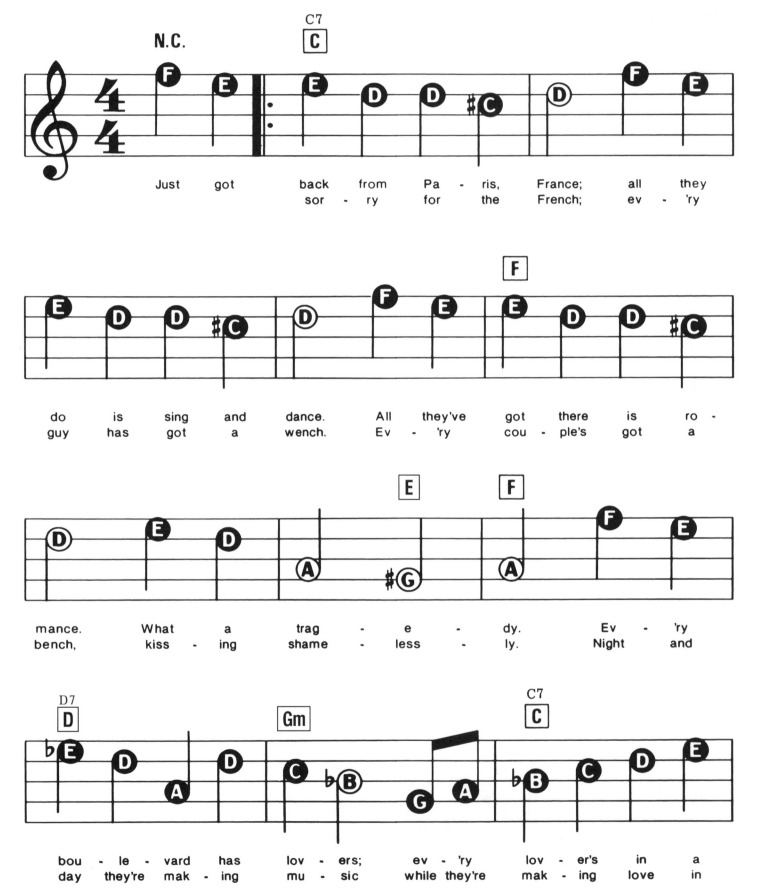

Just got back from Pa - ris, France; all they
sor - ry for the French; ev - 'ry

do is sing and dance. All they've got there is ro -
guy has got a wench. Ev - 'ry cou - ple's got a

mance. What a trag - e - dy. Ev - 'ry
bench, kiss - ing shame - less - ly. Night and

bou - le - vard has lov - ers; ev - 'ry lov - er's in a
day they're mak - ing mu - sic while they're mak - ing love in

51

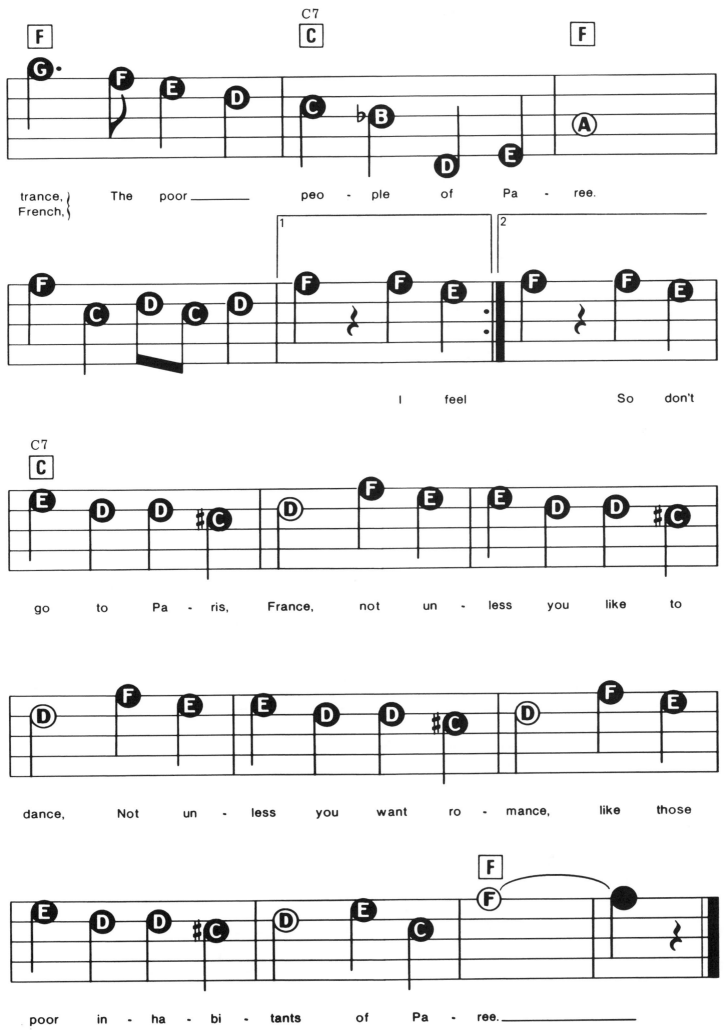

Under Paris Skies

English Words by Kim Gannon
French Words by Jean Drejac
Music by Hubert Giraud

Registration 10
Rhythm: Waltz

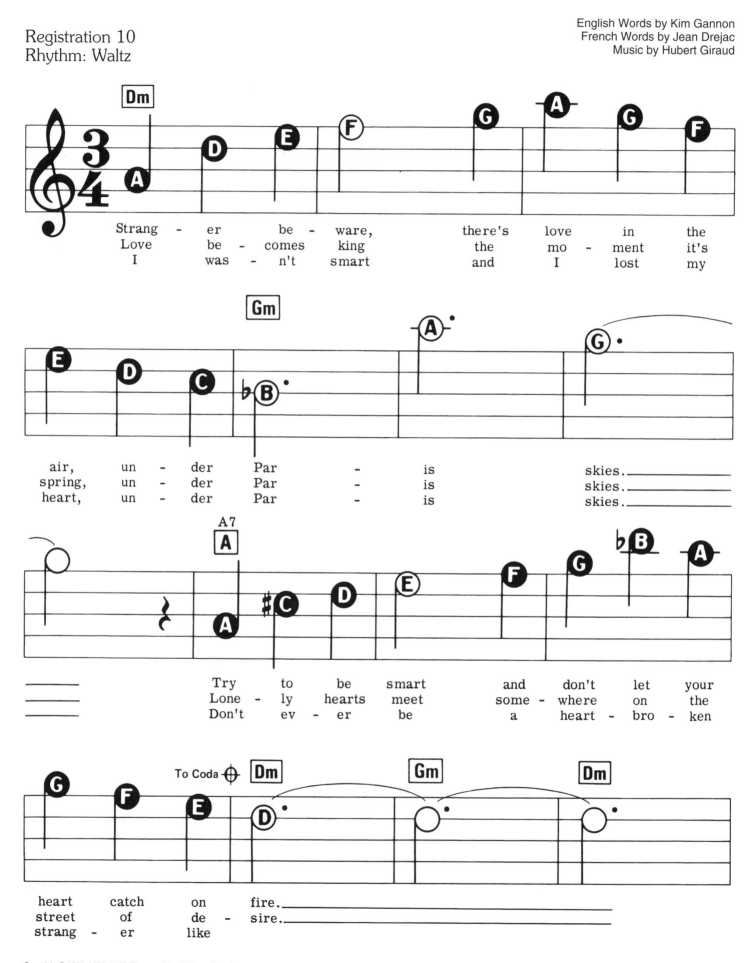

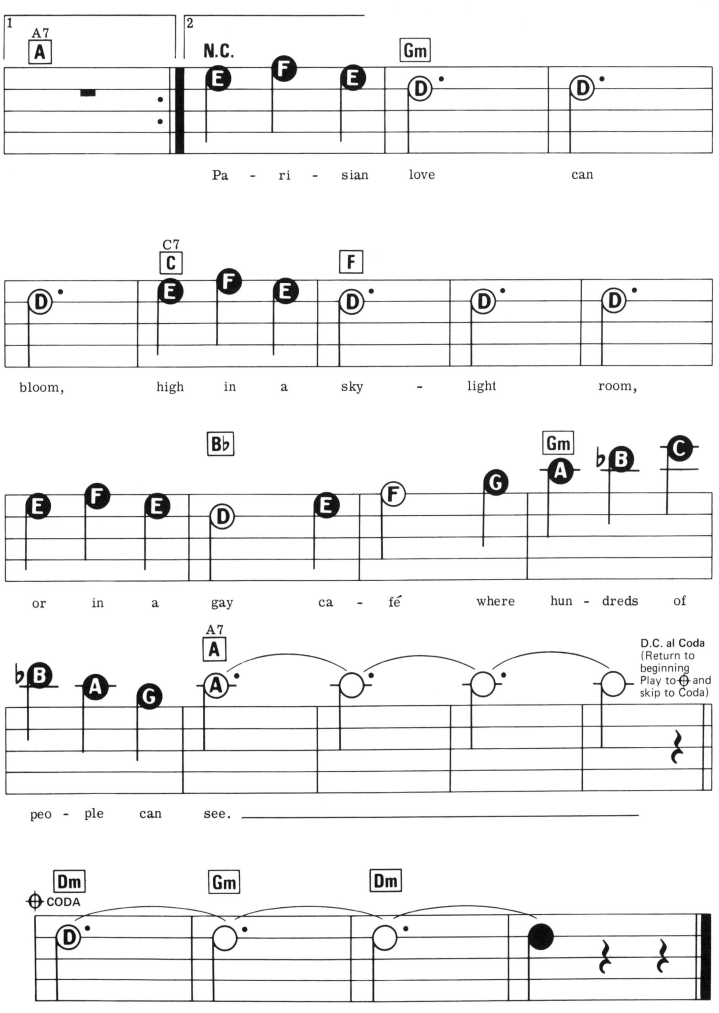

Watch What Happens
from THE UMBRELLAS OF CHERBOURG

Registration 2
Rhythm: Bossa Nova or Latin

Music by Michel Legrand
Original French Text by Jacques Demy
English Lyrics by Norman Gimbel

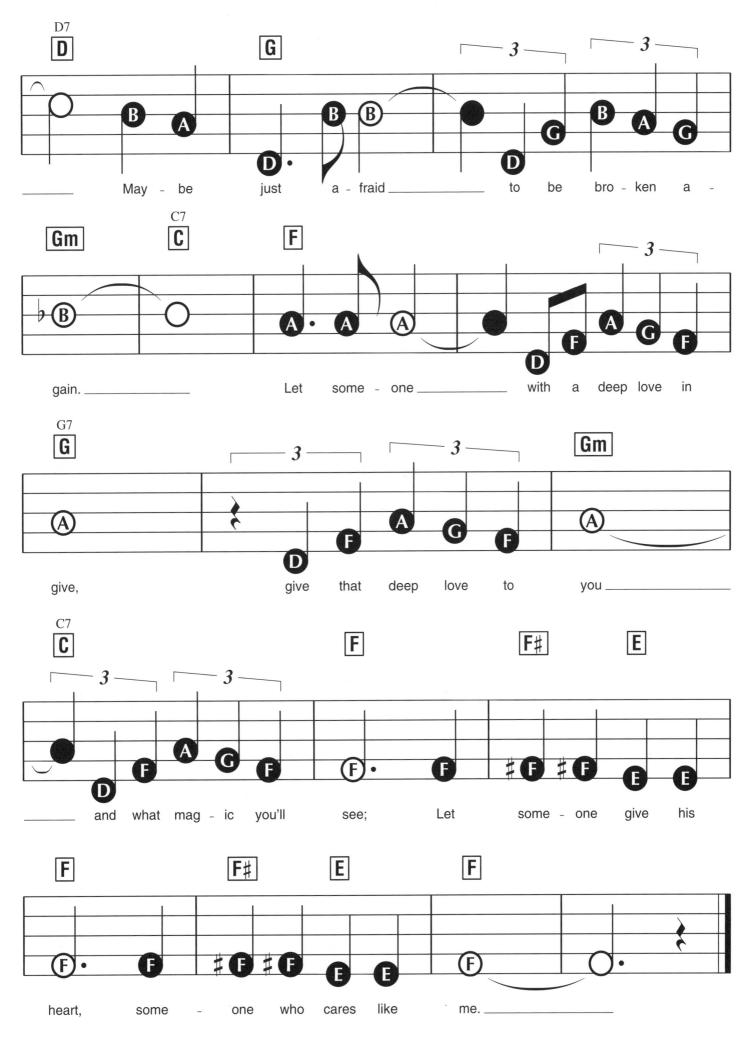

What Now My Love
(Et maintenant)

Registration 2
Rhythm: Swing

Original French Lyric by Pierre Delano
Music by Francois Becaud
English Adaptation by Carl Sigman

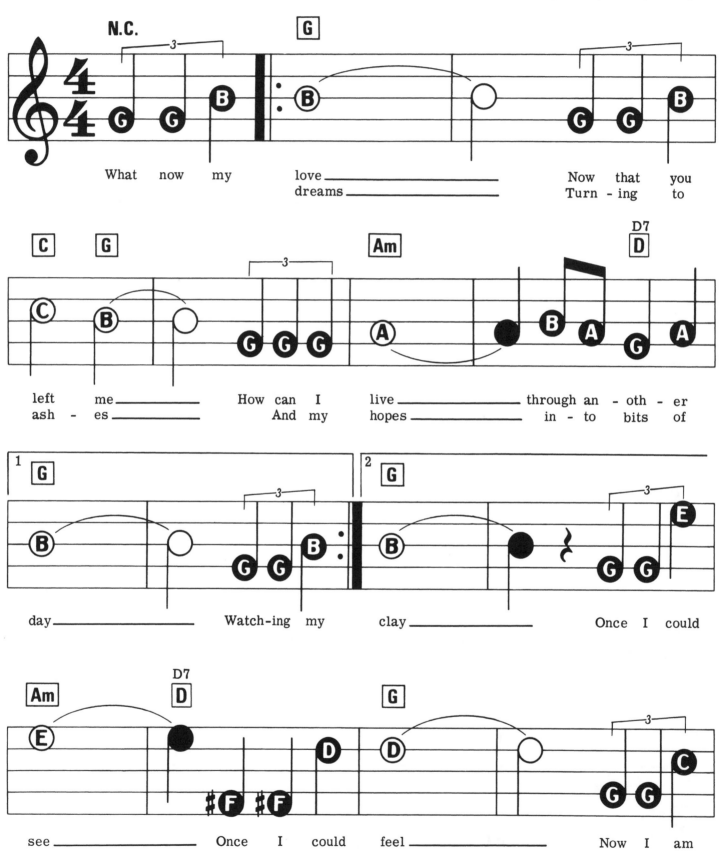

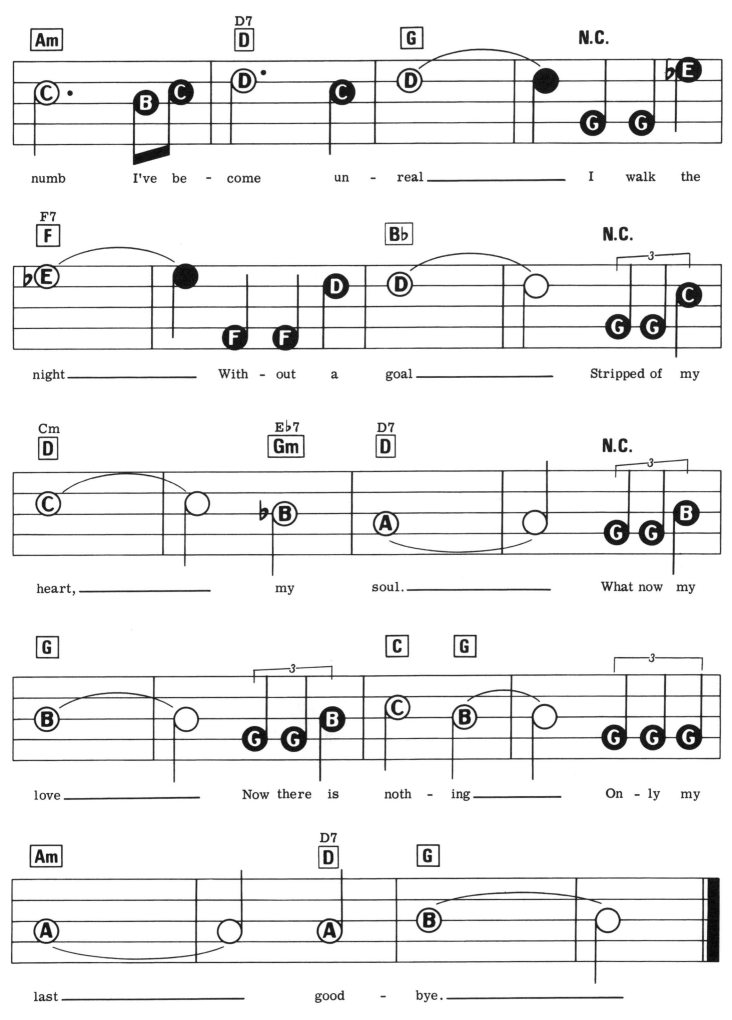

Where Is Your Heart
(The Song from Moulin Rouge)
from MOULIN ROUGE

Registration 2
Rhythm: Waltz

Words by William Engvick
Music by George Auric

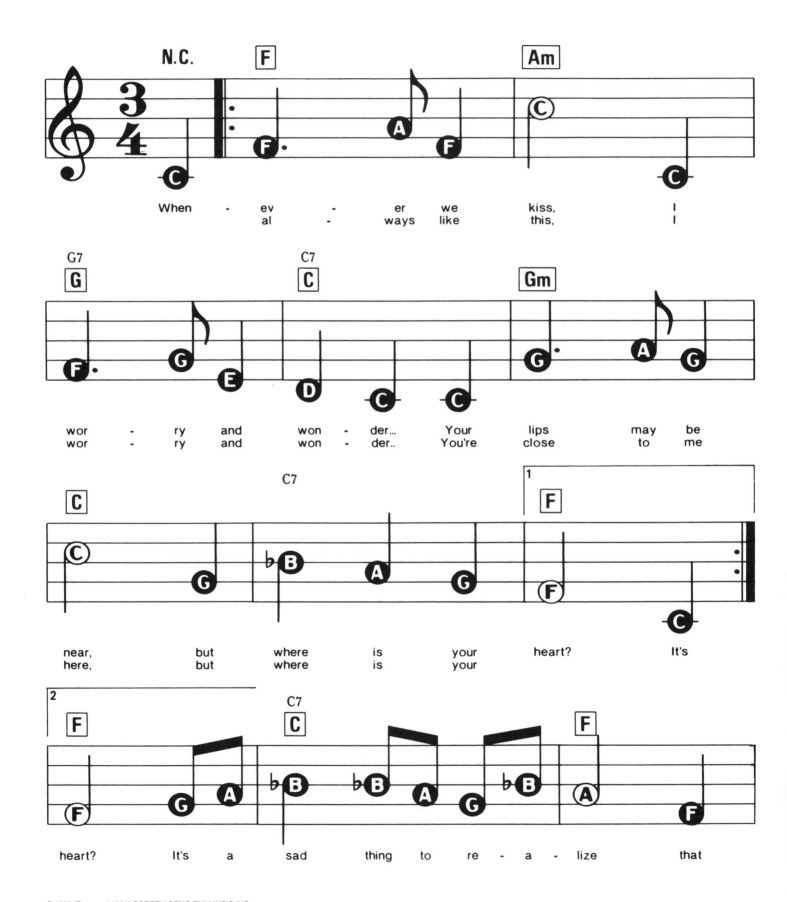

Padam Padam

Registration 3
Rhythm: Waltz

Words by Henri Contet
Music by Norbert Glanzberg

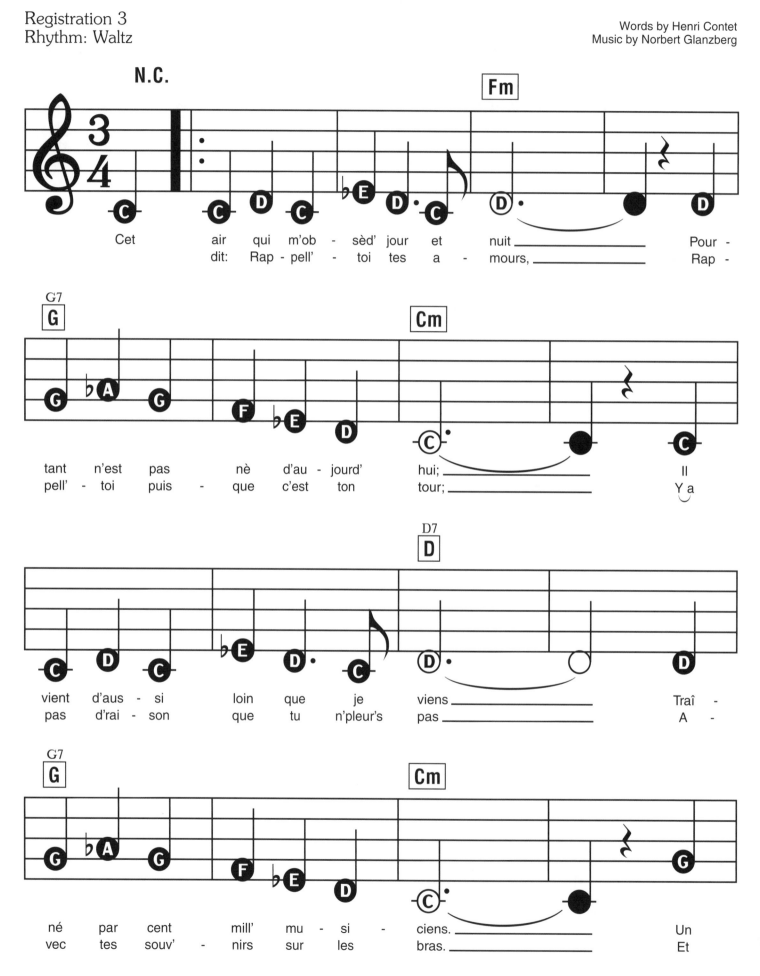

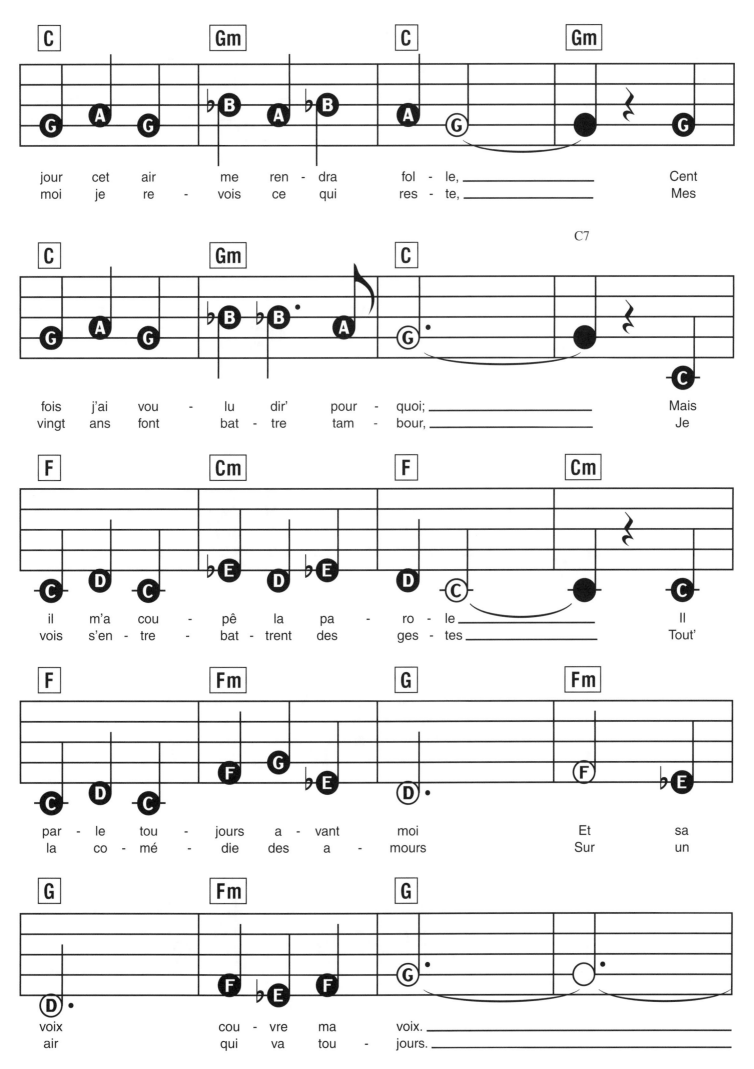

62

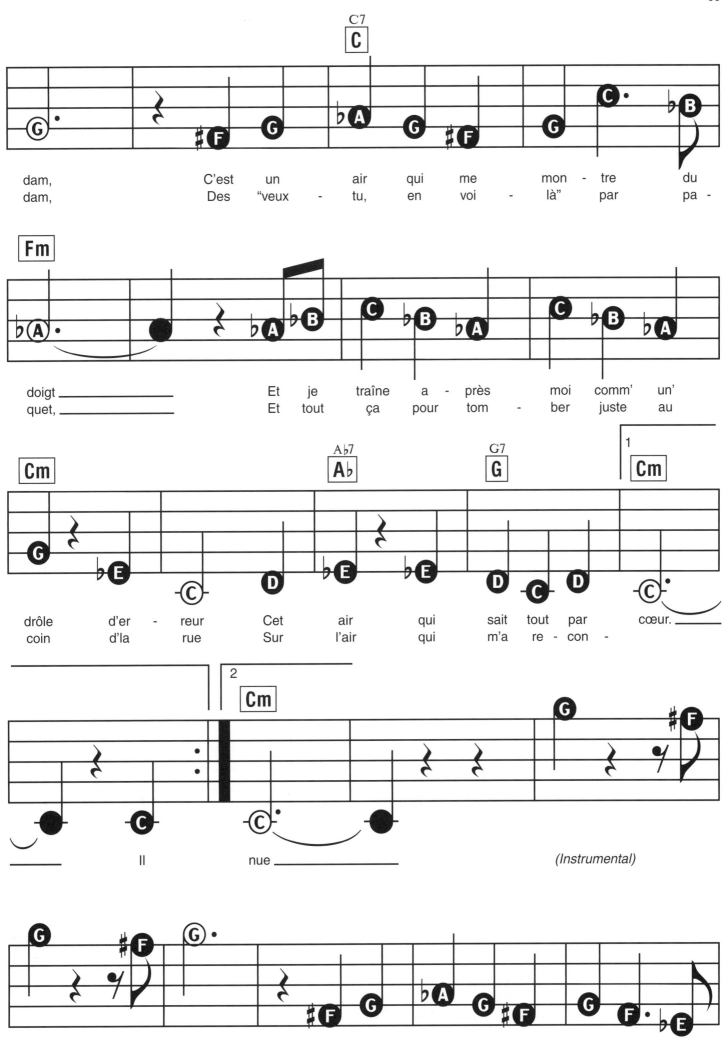

dam,   C'est   un   air   qui   me   mon - tre   du
dam,   Des   "veux - tu,   en   voi - là"   par   pa -

doigt _____   Et   je   traîne   a - près   moi comm' un'
quet, _____   Et   tout   ça   pour tom - ber   juste au

drôle   d'er - reur   Cet   air   qui   sait tout par   cœur. _____
coin   d'la   rue   Sur   l'air   qui   m'a   re - con -

_____   Il   nue _____   (Instrumental)

                                                                    E - cou - tez le cha - hut qu'il me

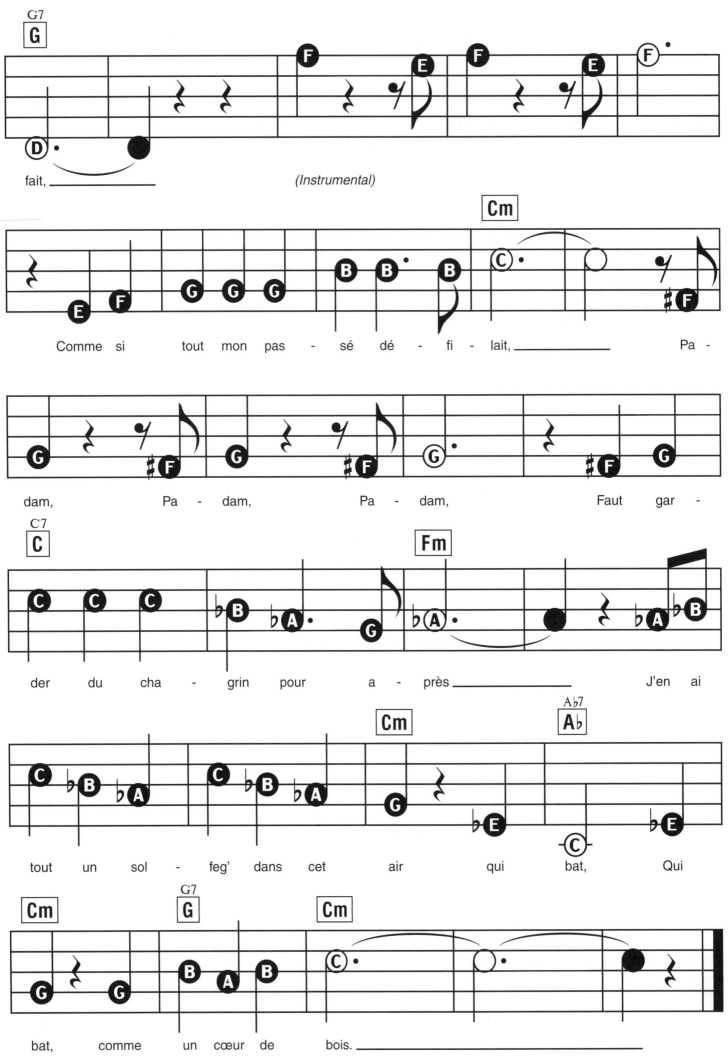

(Instrumental)

fait, _____

Comme si tout mon pas - sé dé - fi - lait, _____ Pa -

dam, Pa - dam, Pa - dam, Faut gar -

der du cha - grin pour a - près _____ J'en ai

tout un sol - feg' dans cet air qui bat, Qui

bat, comme un cœur de bois. _____